LIFE AT HOME IN THE TWENTY-FIRST CENTURY

The Jo Anne Stolaroff Cotsen Prize Imprint
honors outstanding studies in archaeology
to commemorate a special person whose
appreciation for scholarship was recognized
by all whose lives she touched.

LIFE AT HOME IN THE TWENTY-FIRST CENTURY

32 FAMILIES OPEN THEIR DOORS

JEANNE E. ARNOLD
ANTHONY P. GRAESCH
ENZO RAGAZZINI
ELINOR OCHS

TABLE OF CONTENTS

This book is set in Scala Sans and Gotham.
Design by Eric Gardner and Jeanne E. Arnold
Photo credits: CELF
Panoramas composed by Enzo Ragazzini; Maps by Anthony P. Graesch

Library of Congress Cataloging-in-Publication Data

Arnold, Jeanne E.
Life at home in the twenty-first century: 32 familes open their doors / Jeanne E. Arnold...[et.al.].
    p.cm.
Includes bibliographical references.
ISBN 978-1-931745-61-1 (hardcover)
1. Material culture--California--Los Angeles--History--21st century. 2. Los Angeles (Calif.)--Social life and customs--21st century. 3. Ethnoarchaeology--California--Los Angeles. 4. Families--California--Los Angeles--History--21st century. 5. Home--California--Los Angeles--History--21st century. 6. Dwellings--California--Los Angeles--History--21st century. I. Title.

GN560. U6A67 2013
392.3'6--dc23

2012011283

ACKNOWLEDGMENTS

This book centers on the material worlds of American families just like yours (and ours). It is the archaeology of today, exploring houses and yards and the thousands of things we acquire and treasure. It is about the way we use our homes, what we cook for dinner, and how we interact with our families each day. It documents the heights of our consumerism and our appetites for new technologies.

The authors are indebted to the 32 California families who participated in this study. By opening their homes and sharing their lives, they demonstrated great trust and hospitality. Their willingness to engage in the project has resulted in a historic and unprecedented study of middle-class American families.

Life at Home emerged from a larger interdisciplinary and collaborative research endeavor by the Center on Everyday Lives of Families (CELF) at UCLA. CELF was funded from 2001 to 2010 by the Alfred P. Sloan Foundation program on the Workplace, Workforce, and Working Families. Our deep thanks go to Kathleen Christensen of the Sloan Foundation for her extraordinary vision and support. Additional information about CELF may be found at www.celf.ucla.edu.

We gratefully acknowledge the fieldwork, transcribing, data management, analyses, and technical assistance of the entire CELF research team. We single out two individuals without whom this book could not have come to full fruition: Paul Connor, computer guru, who more than once brought CELF's massive data archives back from the brink, and Eric Gardner, whose fine design work has been instrumental in bringing our vision to the printed page.

The CELF faculty include authors Elinor Ochs (Director of the CELF center) and Jeanne E. Arnold, along with Thomas Bradbury, Linda Garro, Charles Goodwin, Marjorie Harness Goodwin, Kris Gutierrez, and Rena Repetti. Our faculty colleagues consistently extended their encouragement and enthusiasm for this part of the larger project, and it was our great fortune to work with them. We are also grateful to Tamar Kremer-Sadlik, director of research for CELF, who has been absolutely instrumental in the success of the many moving parts of the overall CELF enterprise, most certainly including this one.

Many CELF postdoctoral fellows, graduate students, staff, and close associates have provided advice and feedback, gathered data, or assisted in any number of ways in the research for this book: Anna Antoniou, Margaret Beck, Julie Bernard, Mara Buchbinder, Belinda Campos, Alessandro Duranti, Mario Fois, Rachel George, Jeffrey Good, Drew Hand, Carolina Izquierdo, Wendy Klein, Tali Klima, Ursula Lang, April Leininger, Heather Loyd, Rachael Madore, Adrian Meza, Angie Mittman, Alesia Montgomery, Scotti Norman, Angela Orlando, Diana Pash, Amy Paugh, Elisa Pigeron, Tatyana Plaksina, Bettie Ras, Johanna Romero, Darby Saxbe, Merav Shohet, Karen Gainer Sirota, Jacqueline Sperling, Eve Tulbert, Aleksandra Van Loggerenberg, Heather Willihnganz, Leah Wingard, Shu-wen Yang, and Kristin Yarris. Colleagues at our sister centers in Italy and Sweden (iCELF and sCELF) also provided valuable perspectives from beyond the U.S. cultural context. Finally, we are grateful to many colleagues, but particularly Michael B. Schiffer, David Hurst Thomas, and Willeke Wendrich, for their reviews and suggestions that helped in situating this project within global research traditions on modern material culture.

ABOUT THE AUTHORS

Jeanne E. Arnold is Professor of Anthropology at the University of California, Los Angeles. At UCLA's Center on Everyday Lives of Families (CELF), she investigates material culture and uses of space at houses in contemporary California. Arnold also directs archaeological field investigations at sites in coastal California and has collaborated on international field projects in British Columbia and Europe. Selected books include *Emergent Complexity, The Origins of a Pacific Coast Chiefdom: The Chumash of the Channel Islands*, and *California's Ancient Past* (with M. Walsh).

Anthony P. Graesch is Assistant Professor of Anthropology at Connecticut College, where he engages students in studies of material culture and built space. He is a founding member of the CELF team, and his research appears in a wide spectrum of social science journals and edited volumes and includes numerous collaborations with linguistic anthropologists, psychologists, and sociologists. Ongoing projects include an ethnoarchaeological study of smoking in public urban spaces and field investigations on households, political economies, and formation processes in British Columbia, where he collaborates with Stó:lo-Coast Salish scholars and community members.

Enzo Ragazzini resides in the Tuscany region of Italy. His photography combines optical, mechanical, and chemical aspects of photography with original perceptions of the human experience in the natural and cultural environment. Ragazzini documents material culture, human labor, communication, visual perception, and modes of transportation around the world. Publications include *The Tropics Before the Engine, Mediterraneo, I Giorni le Opere (The Days, the Work)*, and *Behind the Scenes of a Great Project: The Making of High Velocity*. His work has been featured at exhibitions in Montreal, London, Oxford, Venice, Milan, New York, and Rome.

Elinor Ochs is UCLA Distinguished Professor of Anthropology and Applied Linguistics and served as Director of the UCLA Sloan Center on Everyday Lives of Families. Ochs examines socioculturally organized communicative practices that apprentice children into how to think, feel, and act in the world. Honors include Fellow of the American Academy of Arts and Sciences (1998–present), MacArthur Fellow (1998–2003), and Guggenheim Fellow (1984). Selected books include *Linguaggio e Cultura, Living Narrative, Constructing Panic*, and *Culture and Language Development*.

01 Life at Home in the Twenty-First Century

For us to really understand how we are similar to, or different from, our ancestors, we must be able to look at ourselves in ways which are comparable to the way we look at past societies (Rathje 1981:54).

THE HOUSES we live in and the domestic objects we own—large, small, costly, inexpensive—define who we are and reveal much about our social identities, family histories, aesthetic preferences, behavioral patterns, affiliations, and economic standing. Yet the staggeringly complex material worlds of contemporary American families have never been systematically documented. We know from our own daily experiences that most U.S. families acquire and interface with many diverse possessions at home, but the leading social scientists of our day (anthropologists, economists, consumer specialists, sociologists) have little idea how families actually use their home spaces, where they situate their old and new stuff, or how many objects they accumulate behind closed doors over the years. Marketers and credit card companies record and analyze every nuance of consumer purchasing patterns, but once people shuttle shopping bags into their homes, the information flow grinds to a halt. How do people interact with these household objects in everyday life? Which objects do they find meaningful? Are Americans burdened by their material worlds? Which key spaces inside the house serve as the main stages on which U.S. family activities unfold? The only way to find out in any rich, textured way is through systematic observation.

Life at Home presents a visual ethnography of middle-class American households, dateline AD 2001–2005, southern California. Two of us (Arnold and Graesch), steeped in traditional archaeological methods, developed the framework of this project along with an anthropologist (Ochs) richly experienced in ethnographic and linguistic studies of family dynamics in Samoa, Madagascar, and the U.S., and an anthropologically oriented photographer (Ragazzini) who has captured striking images of people around the globe. The result of this multi-year collaboration is an unvarnished view of the home lives of contemporary families and their material possessions in depth and in real time. Our enterprise draws on a newly developed archive of 20,000 digital images, dozens of maps, thousands of scanned observations, and 1,500 hours of videotaped daily activities at 32 Los Angeles–area homes.

A few tantalizing efforts to examine these kinds of data precede us, each addressing some fragment of the whole and originating from distinct research traditions. Psychologists Csikszentmihalyi and Rochberg-Halton, in their 1981 book *The Meaning of Things*, provided foundational details about which of their possessions middle-class Americans most deeply value. As is customary in the broader social sciences, their research involved self reports from a large sample of families who answered questionnaires and surveys. The results were instrumental in documenting American attitudes of that era about objects in the domestic sphere, but for our purposes, the small range of object types (about 15) and the number of families (4) they directly observed were limiting.

Panoramas stitched together from 12–18 individual images capture the full span of a home's main rooms. This is a panorama of a Los Angeles family room.

In recent decades, sociologists, economists, and consumer historians have used quantitative and qualitative methods (most often very large-scale surveys and self reports) to investigate how people spend their money and their time in today's harried "work-and-spend" and "shop-til-you-drop" society. Juliet Schor is among those leading the way in this important research, exposing the sheer scale of consumerism in the U.S. and, by extension, prompting us to think about just how much stuff winds up in American houses. These studies do not, however, tell us what families actually do with their possessions, nor what they keep, display, store, use, and discard each day. Large-scale surveys also provide little if any information about attitudes and interactions regarding family possessions.

History tells us that western post-Renaissance societies (Europe, North America) have deep-rooted traditions embracing homes and possessions as central to personal identities, albeit to quite varying degrees. Intricate histories of housing and consumer trends penned by Thorstein Veblen (*The Theory of the Leisure Class*), Judith Flanders (*Inside the Victorian Home*), Dolores Hayden (*Redesigning the American Dream*), Clare Cooper Marcus (*The House As a Mirror of Self*), and others portray shifting philosophies over the last two centuries about the house as a repository for memories and prized things. Periods of competitive domestic display cycle in and out of favor, although it is

evident that nothing in the past has approached the breadth and intensity of early 2000s American consumption and material signaling. Consumer-oriented societies also tend to spawn widespread collecting of objects, from beer cans to rare coins to fine art. We all know people who collect; indeed, most U.S. households have a collector, even if it is a child collecting shells or stamps. In the engaging *Collecting in a Consumer Society*, Russell Belk explores the propensity for those living in object-rich societies to assemble special collections. His vignettes depict diverse personal motivations for collecting, but Belk links the pattern on a holistic level to flourishing consumerism.

Further tracing the historical roots of competitive consumerism in the U.S., psychiatrist Peter Whybrow documents an American "mania" to consume, which results in overwork, overspending, and over-accumulating. He links the highs of manic consumerism to serious outcomes for families: not only bankruptcy and massive credit debt but also physiological stress and a sense of failure as the American dream goes awry. And in documentaries, books, and articles, dozens of other researchers from Annie Leonard (*The Story of Stuff*) and Peter Stearns (*Consumerism in World History*) to Robert Frank (*Luxury Fever*) detail the toll exacted on American parents by excessive consumption and the manipulations of children by advertisers seeking to hook youngsters into long-term brand allegiances for cereals,

fast foods, and electronics. One stunning measure of the real burden of materialism can be found in the results of a OnePoll survey of 2,000 women, which reveals that a typical U.S. female spends more than 25,184 hours shopping for household essentials during her lifetime (equivalent to 24 hours per day for nearly three years—not counting discretionary shopping).

These contributions bring attention to the domestic material world. But almost never have scientists gone into U.S. houses to see and independently document domestic life or the material consequences of any of these phenomena. During the 1960s, one pioneering sociologist tallied objects in Detroit living rooms and linked material choices to consumption trends, and a second scholar documented fine art in New York City households, but the potential of this research went largely unrecognized.

As we were developing this project, Peter Menzel's *Material World* was opening eyes to conspicuous differences in degrees of affluence and people's attitudes about belongings around the globe. His photographs depict all of the major possessions of one household apiece from 30 of the 183 member countries in the United Nations. Everything these families own was lugged outside and assembled in their front yards with the family members standing by. As fascinating as these images are, they are unsatisfying from an archaeological

perspective because the objects are removed from their normal behavioral and spatial contexts—they are no longer *in situ*. We do not see where the families chose to situate these possessions, how they use them, which hold prominent positions for display, or how they or the rooms they were in shape behavior. This is ironic since the book otherwise attracts attention to the ways that material culture powerfully conveys information about cultural identity.

Several of the world's most distinguished photographers have spent their careers taking remarkable images of people and their homes and possessions. Those most attuned to the visual interplay between what people own and who they are have also influenced the way our study unfolded and the images we present here. Walker Evans in the 1930s and Bill Owens in the 1960s are among the photographers who have portrayed the lives and homes of ordinary people with a sensitive anthropological eye. Another is Frederic Brenner, who visited the homes of Jewish people all over the world and took informative, probing photographs of the house interiors. These images, rich in emotion and a sense of place and time, are a world apart from recent commercial projects that survey days in the life of "America" or "Maine" or depict how randomly selected Americans live at home. Although they appeal to our basic curiosity about our neighbors, these popular coffee table volumes have neither a scientific approach with explanatory goals nor melded artistic/anthropological sensibilities.

The interior of a
Northwest Coast
plank house on
Vancouver Island,
featuring hearth,
cooking area,
and possessions.
Illustration by John
Webber, 1752–1793.
*Interior of Habitation
at Nootka Sound.*

Courtesy of the Peabody
Museum of Archaeology
and Ethnology, Harvard
University, 41-72-10/499.

LIFE AT HOME

Projecting that we and other researchers will mine the
data for decades to come, our project design encompasses
the broad and systematic collection of data with an eye
to a whole range of questions that might be asked. As a
result, the photographs taken at each house in the study
are comprehensive rather than merely selective and
idiosyncratic, and we recorded data on how people use
their time on a rigorous schedule whether or not people
appeared to be doing anything of immediate interest.

The research design for this enormous endeavor is, of course,
multi-dimensional, and we closely investigate a number
of specific anthropological questions. Among them we
examine how possessions concentrated in specific house
spaces function as organizational or mnemonic devices;
which household artifacts families use most frequently to
construct and express personal and family identity, and
where they display them; and how remodeling choices and
family investments in parts of the home tie in with cultural
ideals. The data needed to address these and other questions
derive from field observations that we conducted at not just

a single home but at 32 southern California households. We
recognize that among social sciences that regularly rely on
survey and self-report methods for describing demographic
and behavioral trends, such a sample seems small. But
within the ethnographic tradition of collecting a wealth of
detailed, nuanced information about everyday interactions and
behavior, 32 households is nearly unprecedented. Even among
archaeological studies, data sets addressing nearly complete
material assemblages for dozens of houses are very rare.

As the twenty-first century arrived, our team of UCLA
scientists began a 4-year-long field project to document the
rich fabric of daily life at home among busy dual-income
middle-class parents and their children. We located 32
families in the greater Los Angeles area who shared our
vision of the importance of this enterprise. They agreed to
open their doors and their lives to a week of filming and
detailed photography of their houses and possessions. The
participating families live in many different neighborhoods
of the city and are ethnically diverse. They all have school-age
children, and they self-identify as middle class, although their
family incomes vary significantly. They are all homeowners,
and thus free to remodel and decorate as they please. We

hear their voices throughout this volume as they comment on their homes, their lives, and their material worlds.

As we would expect in typical middle-class neighborhoods everywhere in the U.S., these parents represent many different occupations, including teachers, firefighters, nurses, dentists, small business owners, social workers, airline pilots, restaurant managers, accountants, lawyers, and contractors. They live in homes that range from modest (under 1,000 square feet) to comfortably large (more than 3,000 square feet). The households in this study include 30 headed by mother-father pairs and 2 headed by two fathers. As owners of their homes, each family is shouldering a monthly mortgage. Both parents in each family work at paid jobs at least 30 hours per week, and more than half report working 40 to 49 hours weekly. One-third of the men and 13 percent of the women find themselves working 50 hours or more. Mothers and fathers range in age from 28 to 58 years. These couples have been together for 3 to 18 years. They are busy raising two or three children who range in age from 1 to 17, and because we wanted to target households with young children, all families have at least one child who is 7 to 12 years old.

ETHNOARCHAEOLOGY / MODERN MATERIAL CULTURE

Archaeologists traditionally excavate houses and cities of ancient populations, mapping and bringing into relief their spaces and artifacts. Detailed analyses of many classes of objects gradually come together to produce a picture of everyday practices and institutions of the inhabitants. The current study employs a simple set of time-tested archaeological and observational methods to record and then critically analyze the domestic material world of U.S. households today. Because twenty-first century America is the most materially affluent society in global history, this is a uniquely data-rich enterprise.

Our material culture approach to American family life emerges from a five-decades-old heritage of ethnoarchaeological research. Ethnoarchaeology builds on the behavioral emphasis of ordinary archaeology—the fundamental interest in reconstructing a broad range of daily behaviors in the past, from making clothing and fashioning tools to processing food for meals. Because archaeologists cannot observe such past behaviors directly, they must develop

A kitchen interior during meal preparation, Los Angeles.

Top left: One family's dining table primed for dinner, play, and homework.
Bottom left: Children's things occupy considerable space in the living rooms of many homes.
Right: A large collection of books, toys, games, and music in a playroom.

sophisticated inferences that link specific patterns of objects (distributions of stone tools or potsherds, for example) and human actions. To do this well, archaeologists need to explore human activities and various taphonomic (e.g., decay) and site formation processes that operate to bring such patterning into existence. Enter ethnoarchaeology, or the ethnographic study of living people and their material worlds for the purpose of better understanding the links between behavior and material culture.

During the 1970s, Lewis Binford decided to live for several months among the Nunamiut, who are semi-nomadic Inupiaq Eskimo caribou hunters in northwestern Alaska. He wanted to learn about basic life activities of hunter-gatherer peoples, including how they set up camp, prepared food, and interacted around the fire. He recorded many details about how they built their seasonal dwellings, where they made their stone tools, how they prepared caribou meat for storage, and where they shared stories and engaged socially. Among other findings, he noted precisely when and where objects were discarded at the hunting camp at the time of its abandonment. These kinds of observations allow scholars

to link the spatial patterning of objects that were lost or tossed out during everyday activities at hunting camps with similar material remains found at ancient encampments in comparable environments.

Several influential ethnoarchaeological studies followed Binford's, and notably, a few of them turned directly to the exploration of domestic settings, including Susan Kent's cross-cultural analyses of household activities in the American Southwest and Africa; Robert Janes's study of house layout and activities among people in the western Canadian subarctic; and other work in households from Iran to South Africa. Each study exemplifies the utility of detailed mapping and ethnographic observation of people in their home environments.

At about the same time that Binford was tracking activity around Nunamiut campfires, Michael Schiffer, William Rathje, Richard Gould, and colleagues in Arizona were embarking on an equally interesting journey: the archaeology of us. Modern material culture studies in the U.S. and other industrial nations occupy a special place within the practice of ethnoarchaeology. Such studies are often in urban locales—and are thus most useful for testing archaeological principles about city life—but they share the fundamental methods of the field: direct observations of human activity in relation to materials and built spaces; questionnaires and interviews; and the recovery, documentation, and interpretation of material remains from houses, trash bins, municipal dumps, and other settings. Pioneering scholars of modern material culture also recognized that the material richness of U.S. society—the proliferation of rapidly changing brands and models of cars since the 1920s, for example, or TVs since the 1950s—is perfect for testing archaeological principles relating to fundamental methods such as seriation.

The roots of our endeavor to study the material world of modern American families at home can be traced to these innovative efforts focusing the analytical lens of ethnoarchaeology on our own society. The best known of these projects began in 1972 as a training exercise for Rathje's University of Arizona archaeology students. In what was later dubbed "The Garbage Project," Tucson-based archaeologists set out to better understand the relationship of modern-day Americans to the objects they discarded as trash. They wanted to know what could be learned about the habits of American consumers from the objects in the family waste bin. How much refuse did the average household contribute annually to city landfills? How did households react to fluctuations in food prices? In a body of research now popularly known as garbology, archaeologists explored these and other questions by first asking homeowners participating in the study about their habits through surveys and interviews. Then the researchers carefully documented the contents of participants' garbage bins.

Rathje's team was able to identify ways in which people's characterizations of their everyday routines deviated from the story told by objects in the household trash. They found that families typically underreported consumption habits that were moralized by their peers, such as imbibing beer and eating red meat. The kinds of things tossed in the garbage provided insight into actual purchasing decisions, dietary choices, and rates of food consumption, all valuable data. We learned important lessons about disparities between what we say we do—our perceptions of our everyday behavior—and what our otherwise silent trash says we actually do.

When people are part of the research equation, modern material culture scholars can ask them to directly

Sisters sharing a bedroom.

discuss in which ways and how often they use their possessions and their built environments; they can ask people to convey how they feel about them; then the material record and the narratives can be compared in any number of ways. During the early 1970s, Schiffer and his Arizona students conducted a series of small-scale studies in western U.S. households on topics ranging from how households recycled/reused household goods such as furniture, to where children did their homework (bedrooms versus dining room tables), to supermarket shopping practices, to roadside dumping patterns.

Our Los Angeles study follows in these traditions, blending traditional archaeological methods with the application of modern material culture approaches to contemporary houses and family life. Our research design called for mapping, intensive photography of virtually everything material in people's homes, and house history questionnaires, while also hearing directly from various family members about their houses during self-narrated home video tours and directly observing and filming them as they prepared meals, used objects, and made complex use of their homes. The information we recovered is systematic rather than anecdotal or confined to single cases so as to maximize its explanatory power. This is one way in which the present study differs significantly from post-processual projects on modern material culture. We have captured at length the voices of our

Top left: A cluttered garage with second refrigerator for surplus food storage. Bottom left: Family photos, magnets, key phone numbers, and schedules are typically displayed on the refrigerator. Right: The kitchen is often the nexus of a range of family activities.

participants and their personal, idiosyncratic utterances about what various objects and rooms mean to them—essential to our interpretations—but we also have robust and wide-ranging assemblages of systematic observational data drawn from our 32 in-depth cases.

Thousands of artifacts fill the modern American house, from major furniture pieces to small and moveable objects such as documents and clothing. Individual objects as well as the assemblages as a whole relay information about the choices and desires of family members who make purchases and decide what to keep and use. The images in this volume show that a spotlight on the material world can generate important insights regarding twenty-first century acquisition preferences, taste, intensity of consumerism, organization, tolerance for clutter, housecleaning habits, and parents' indulgence of children's demands for playthings.

Our field methods systematically capture how people of different ages and genders interact with these possessions and move through their rooms. Only very rarely would such

information come to us from the ancient world. The closest we might get is the great volcanic eruption at Pompeii, Italy, which in just minutes buried a whole city and its people in their homes and plazas. But even Pompeii is only a snapshot of one moment in time; fantastic as it is, the preserved city cannot reveal what people were doing days or months before that moment or how they used their homes and artifacts over the course of many days.

Archaeologists use meticulous approaches to interpret sparse and fragmented data from house remains of past societies; here, we have the luxury of exploring much more abundantly stocked domestic settings and examining our own familiar surroundings in a new light. Since our study of the everyday material worlds of U.S. households has the resources to expand the scope and interpretive reach of today's best modern material culture research, we apply this highly meticulous approach to all aspects of our data collection. We catalogued the visible possessions in every room of the 32 households and documented their uses, noting counts of artifacts, the richness and diversity of

A home office with high densities of possessions, including business and school documents, photo albums, media electronics, and sports memorabilia.

things owned, where objects are placed, what happens when households accumulate too many things, which rooms are used and not used, and how time at home is spent. We itemized what and when family members eat, where and when they interact, and how they divide their time across chores and leisure. We recorded their thoughts and feelings about what their homes mean to them and how they experience stress when their homes are cluttered or in the midst of remodeling.

REAL-TIME OBSERVATIONS IN UNSTAGED HOMES

Americans have grown accustomed to a high level of familial privacy, a perspective that produces few opportunities for scientists or others to glimpse unstaged life behind closed doors of ordinary neighborhoods. Glossy architectural publications feature the ostentatious and professionally decorated houses of celebrities and the wealthy, but of course photographers and homeowners carefully choose what to show. The spaces are staged and

tidied. This volume is the counterpoint to those images: an unflinching examination of actual homes amid all of the joys and messiness of real life. The photographs usher us into the intimate spaces of homes replete with each family's unique selection of possessions and design choices. We see their unembellished material worlds.

Another important advance we can claim is that we see household artifacts in their place, in situ, something we cannot do at the trash bin or city dump. As Schiffer has shown, each possession has a complex life story, a tale that includes when and where it was made; its acquisition; its placement in the home; its use, including re-purposing or movements around the house; and eventually its removal, which might mean a shift to the garage, a gift to charity, bestowal to a relative, or disposal as trash. Certain possessions (including heirlooms, paintings, and photographs) have special significance in unlocking how people think, act, feel, and organize themselves as a social unit, so we want to know where people place them.

Here we focus not on the life histories of particular objects, but the broad patterns emerging from our analyses of the photographed material assemblages. We also draw heavily on detailed observations of family members' at-home social lives. These aspects of subject and scale distinguish this study from a large corpus of social science research on the behaviors and possessions of dual-earner households with children.

The Alfred P. Sloan Foundation is dedicated to understanding the busy lives of working families in the United States, and the UCLA Center on Everyday Lives of Families (CELF) was established by the Foundation in 2001 to systematically document the experiences and challenges of middle-class, dual-earner parents with school-age children. Our in-depth field study involved naturalistic observations of family life at home through ethnographic video recordings, photography of house spaces and possessions, and sampling of family members' activities at timed intervals. At each house, two ethnographers followed family members with video cameras and a third researcher methodically recorded—every 10

minutes—each family member's location, behavior, and the objects they were using. We call these our scan sampling observations.

CELF team members created an extensive archive of nearly 20,000 photographs and 32 detailed house floor plans. We mapped all indoor and outdoor spaces, including locations of televisions, furniture, and lighting. Parents and older children filmed self-narrated home tours, each individually commenting on rooms, how the family uses the house, favorite possessions, remodeling, art, and any other topic that pertained to the house. We have more than 60 such video narratives from the parents and about 100 overall that we mine for valuable insights regarding family perspectives.

This volume unites scientific and artistic visions of life at home in the twenty-first century. We—two archaeologists, a linguistic anthropologist, and a photographer—selected sets of photographs that most powerfully speak to the contemporary condition in America. Combing through

the thousands of images, all initially taken by project anthropologists with the purpose of creating formal scientific records documenting the homes and objects, we aim to illuminate what is so extraordinary about the ordinary in our material surroundings.

For instance, our homes and possessions organize and define and in some cases engulf us; U.S. hyperconsumerism is most certainly on display. And although the photographs capture the material worlds of a sample of Los Angeles families, this is an issue of global importance, since intensive consumerism has now reached many parts of the world. L.A. is a unique city, just as Chicago and New York and Phoenix are, but this is a pervasive American phenomenon, not a regional one.

A second observation is that distinctive sets of objects that materialize family memories, accomplishments, and affiliations occupy a surprising amount of space in American homes, and other previously unrecognized

assemblages of artifacts that we find aggregated in kitchens function to organize many of the L.A. families' lives and schedules. A third new line of inquiry allows us to see how and where middle-class Angelinos spend their leisure time and reveals how infrequently they find time together inside or in the back yards of their homes.

We present findings primarily in the present tense, but readers should recall that field observations were made between 2001 and 2005. While much remains the same in American households today, in just a few short years we have experienced important shifts in material culture. Two examples are a steady die-off of cathode ray tube televisions and monitors as flat-screen models became affordable and rapid-fire introduction of stylistic and technological variations in cell phones. We have also been affected by the deep 2008 recession and its many impacts on employment, banking, and consumerism. So the "present" is an ethnographic present, situated in 2001–2005.

Bookshelves and a closet filled with a girl's trophies, games, books, and clothes. In the mirror we catch a glimpse of a project team member photographing the room's contents.

A bedroom panorama. The research team classified and counted all visible objects in every room.

THEMES

The rest of this volume explores defining themes of middle-class life at home.

MATERIAL SATURATION: MOUNTAINS OF POSSESSIONS: The intense consumerism that prevailed during the late twentieth century has led to great accumulations of objects that pervade many middle-class U.S. homes and spill out into garages and yards. Amid sometimes extraordinary clutter, families display artifacts that convey their interests and histories: dolls and toys, music and DVDs, family photographs, assorted souvenirs, sports memorabilia, trophies, flags, and more. Our photo archive particularly reveals the ubiquity of children's popular culture, with kids' artifacts found in every corner of the house. We also feature the transformed nature of the middle-class garage as a storage area filled to the rafters and the refrigerator panel as an iconic place that yields information about possessions in the rest of the house.

FOOD, FOOD, FOOD: Visual representations of our eating habits resonate with America's current health concerns (obesity, heart disease, and diabetes) as well as with the perceptions of working parents that they have little time to prepare meals from fresh ingredients. Rarely is the entire family together at mealtimes; weekday dinners are often eaten in stages or in different rooms of the house. Middle-class American families purchase and eat a remarkable array of frozen, canned, and boxed convenience foods and have a propensity to stockpile these foods and related goods to such an extent that they overflow into second refrigerators and garage storage areas.

VANISHING LEISURE: Our detailed analyses of how family members spend their time provide new perspectives on middle-class families' vanishing leisure time at home. While families in L.A. continue to articulate a suburban ideal that emerged in the 1950s that backyards should be centers for "outdoor living," few actually live this way. Parents simply do not find time for outdoor leisure, and most children spend no time at all outside at home even though families have acquired and installed pools, hot tubs, swing sets, trampolines, barbeques, decks, outdoor dining sets, and the like. Leisure is indoors. Most families have cluttered home offices or desk spaces with computers that are visually stress inducing and intrude on indoor leisure time, reminding families of workplace commitments. The material residue of families' vanishing leisure includes these overused home offices and rarely used back yard patios and play areas.

KITCHENS AS COMMAND CENTERS: Twenty-first century kitchens continue the ancient tradition of the hearth as a central locus of domestic life. Photographs, maps, and activity logs show how modern kitchens serve as household command centers from which families coordinate school calendars, work schedules, and the day's events. Documents such as prescriptions, phone numbers, invitations, and event reminders compete for space on the front of the refrigerator. If there is only one wall clock in the house, we find it in this center for family operations. Everyone stores keys, cell phones, chargers, PDAs, backpacks, and lunch boxes on kitchen counters and tables. Parents and children gather frequently at kitchen tables for meals, of course, but also for numerous practical activities such as homework, bill paying, and daily planning.

BATHROOM BOTTLENECKS: Homes built 40 to 70 years ago dominate today's urban landscape but were designed by architects whose visions of family life did not include all of the exigencies of contemporary households. Photographs, floor plans, and video stills illustrate how older homes with fewer than two full bathrooms may impede the flow of daily routines. Single bathrooms are a significant bottleneck in the hectic morning preparations for work and school. Like a busy four-lane road that narrows to two, the bathroom is a contested space through which the routine traffic of morning showers, tooth brushing, hair styling, and other self-care activities must be compressed.

MASTER SUITES AS SANCTUARIES: A major paradox of middle-class family life in the U.S. is that many parents design large master bedroom suites with bathrooms and spacious walk-in closets when they remodel, yet these suites turn out to be the least-used space in the home during waking hours. These "sanctuaries" are envisioned as soothing, spa-like retreats from the stresses of clutter, housework, and raising a family. Although they are underused, in one sense they conform to the ideal: whereas dense accumulations of objects invade other rooms of the house, we find that the suites are kept relatively tidy and uncluttered, suggesting that these spaces are treated differently and hold some positive psychological significance for harried parents.

PLUGGED IN: As is widely recognized, electronic equipment and screen media are ubiquitous in the American home and represent a significant investment of family financial resources. Large-scale surveys by economists and consumer researchers tell us that televisions, computers, gaming consoles, and hand-held game devices are central to domestic life. Our data yield some notably different conclusions and reveal important nuances regarding how these artifacts are really used. Home electronics both isolate and unite family members in work and play.

A boy busy with an array of toys in his bedroom.

MY SPACE, YOUR SPACE, OUR SPACE: The American home is a three-dimensional canvas of personal expression. Although homes in cultures around the globe contain lifetime accumulations of possessions that hold personal meaning, U.S. families take the personalizing of home spaces to another level. Things inherited, things acquired from family travels, and things that represent accomplishments display to family members and others alike who they are and what they like. Walls and shelves are lined with photos, heirlooms, awards, mementos, and children's artwork. Expressions of affiliation with various nations, religions, pop culture icons, and sports heroes are ubiquitous. Children's bedrooms are branded with their names on doors, walls, and furniture.

Perhaps most telling of all, the average L.A. household has dozens of family photos on display throughout the home. According to our CELF colleagues, far less of this kind of personalizing behavior is found in middle-class homes in Europe and South America.

HOW DID WE COLLECT OUR DATA?

The Center on Everyday Lives of Families research team spent a week in the homes of 32 southern California families. Site visits occurred between late 2001 and early 2005. Although these families all self-identify as middle class, they represent many neighborhoods, ethnic groups, occupations, and incomes. Each family that joined the study consists of two parents who both work full time (or close to it), and two or three children, one of whom is 7 to 12 years old. We sought families that were negotiating the many challenges associated with having both parents in the workforce while they were raising young children.

The full scope of the study goes well beyond the material worlds at these homes. We completed extensive videotaping of family life (more than 1,500 hours), conducted interviews about health and social networks, and collected cortisol samples to track highs and lows of stress. The Sloan Foundation supported an experienced research team of linguistic anthropologists, psychologists, archaeologists, medical anthropologists, sociologists, education specialists, and more than 100 students. The CELF website lists journal articles and other publications that emerged from the study, many of which we cite in this volume.

To systematically document our materially oriented data, we adapted several methods from archaeological and observational studies. We requested that each parent and capable child produce a videotaped home-tour narrative, resulting in more than 100 family-narrated home video tours; we recorded all at-home family activities ("scan sampling") at systematic 10-minute intervals; we drafted detailed floor plan maps of the homes, furnishings, and yards; we distributed questionnaires on the home's history (e.g., remodeling events, year built, year bought, storage); and we took thousands of digital photographs of the houses and possessions (see TABLE 1).

DIGITAL PHOTOGRAPHY ARCHIVE: Our emphasis is on photographic documentation of the homes and the lived-in material worlds of families; there are no staged representations of their art or decorations. This is not a "House Beautiful" or "Architectural Digest" presentation of American homes, but a raw look at how people actually live. The images in this volume were captured by social scientists rather than professional photographers, and each was shot with an eye toward thorough documentation of material culture or object-person interaction. We photographed every room, yard, and driveway from multiple angles, ultimately archiving nearly 20,000 images. Images range from systematic wide-angle views capturing full walls and furnishings of a space to close-ups of shelves, mantel displays, the insides of refrigerators, and the contents of closets. Panoramas of interior and exterior spaces, stitched

TABLE 1: HOUSEHOLD DATA*

Detailed house floor plans and lot maps	32
Hours of videotaped family interactions	1,540
Hours of family-narrated video home tours	47
Scan sampling observations	16,935
Digital photographs	19,987
House history questionnaires	32

* *Photographs in this volume are listed on page 162.*

together digitally from 12 to 18 separate images, present the full sweep of a room or yard and convey the emotional impact of the space.

The photo archive allows us to analyze many aspects of household material culture, even years after the conclusion of the fieldwork. We coded 50 main object categories—for example, furniture, computer equipment, book, toy, art —and entered the data in a searchable database. With a few keystrokes, we can find and view all photos containing any particular category of artifacts, assess where particular object types tend to be concentrated, or find out which families have few or many such objects. For a second and much more elaborate coding project, we have used the photo archive to generate full counts of each of roughly 200 object types present in each home, and we have done this for every main household and outdoor space. The resulting database is a goldmine of information about modern life, how we organize our domestic worlds, what choices we make about displaying or storing the things we own, and the scale of today's American consumerism.

FLOOR PLANS: We carefully measured every interior and exterior home space to produce detailed floor plans and maps. We also plotted locations of major furnishings, lighting, built-ins, storage areas, patios, pools, televisions, and other features that tend to shape how people use their homes. These architectural schematics allow us to plot the intensity of family activities space-by-space, showing important disparities in how families use different rooms at home. The floor plans also reveal how configurations of home spaces organize everyday family behavior and interactions.

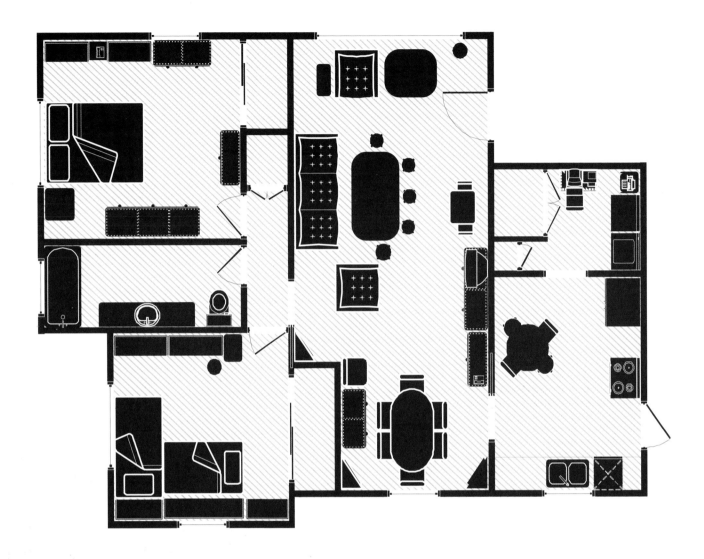

Floor plan of the interior spaces and major furnishings of a two-bedroom house in the study.

SCAN SAMPLING: Our high-resolution scan sampling data sets document how family members move about and use their homes and yards. During our weeklong visits with the families, we systematically observed and recorded the location and activities of each family member every 10 minutes, entering the data into small computing devices preprogrammed with customized activity menus. Our archives contain nearly 17,000 observations for the 32 families, complete with a record of where each person is, what he/she is doing, which artifacts he/she is using, and with whom he/she is interacting.

VIDEO FILMING: The CELF team had two cameras on at all times following the activities of the 32 families. These 1,540 hours of film constitute a wealth of information about family interactions, the character of their relationships, the nature of their daily joys and stresses, and the details of their language use. We occasionally draw on the video data sets to show family activity patterns in various parts of the home.

FAMILY-NARRATED VIDEO HOME TOURS: The voices of the L.A. families are heard directly through the family-narrated video home tours that they made at our request. We supplied a video camera and asked that each

parent (separately) and each child older than about age 7 proceed through the house and yard and, as they film, comment on what the space is, how they use it, what items are of special importance, and any other thoughts they have about the house. The video archive of these home tours includes more than 47 hours of narrative from about 60 parents and 70 children. Some last just a few minutes and tell us relatively little, but others are up to 50 minutes long and provide rich insights into house histories, family tastes and dreams, the meaningfulness of heirloom objects or gifts, special collections made by the family, the stories behind family photos, and the anxiety they may feel about clutter or unfinished remodeling projects. Excerpts from these home tour narratives complement and enrich our observations throughout this volume.

The degree to which we are affected by our domestic environments—the internal configurations of houses and the furnishings and objects in and around them—is frequently underestimated. Residential buildings profoundly shape the behavior of people. Individuals who live in homes of distinct forms and contents internalize a spectrum of spatial and social rules regarding appropriate activities there. They become socialized via cultural norms and kin to be sure, but also through interactions with their furnishings and built surroundings. They learn what to buy and the kinds of behavior that are proper in various rooms.

During the last three decades, scholars have increasingly embraced the archaeology of ancient households, which focuses on these very same phenomena: the full, rich cascade of daily activities. Day-in, day-out behaviors reflect varying family identities and put a particular stamp on the material assemblages of households in different times and places. The data and images in this book document the unique material signatures of 32 twenty-first century California households, but they also reveal underlying characteristics that mark unambiguously American ways of life at home.

Left: A project ethnographer filming one of the Los Angeles families.

Right: The 20,000-photo archive includes many scenes of front and back yard spaces.

ABOUT THE FAMILIES

GEOGRAPHIC DISTRIBUTION

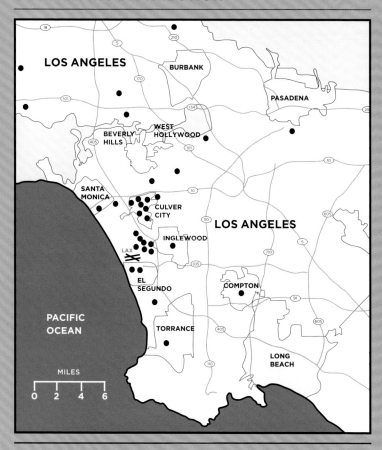

HOUSEHOLD COMPOSITION

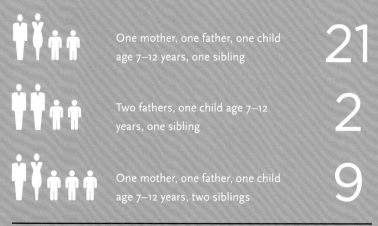

One mother, one father, one child age 7–12 years, one sibling — **21**

Two fathers, one child age 7–12 years, one sibling — **2**

One mother, one father, one child age 7–12 years, two siblings — **9**

MEDIAN AGE

42 Median age of fathers (range = 32–58 years)

41 Median age of mothers (range = 28–50 years)

L.A. AREA NEIGHBORHOODS: SELF-REPORTED

Baldwin Hills
Castle Heights
Compton
Del Rey
El Segundo
Encino
Hancock Park
Heritage Park
Inglewood
La Crescenta
Los Feliz

Redondo Beach
South Pasadena
Southwood (Torrance)
Studio City
Sunkist Park (Culver City)
Sunset Park (Santa Monica)
Valley Glen (Van Nuys)
West Hills
Westchester
Westside (El Segundo)
Westside Village (Culver City)

AGES OF 73 CHILDREN ACROSS 32 FAMILIES

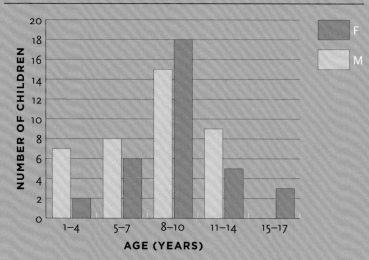

SELF-DESCRIBED CAREERS

Human Resources Manager
General Building Contractor
Clerical Assistant
Company Owner
Category Manager
Ocean Lifeguard   Technician
City Government Chief of Staff
Construction Foreman
Actuarial Analyst
Consultant District Administrator
Deputy Sheriff
Actuary
Acupuncturist   Public Relations
Assistant Registrar   Lawyer
Computer Programmer
Family Childcare Provider
Entrepreneur
Social Worker & Case Manager   Dentist
Classroom Teaching Aide
Executive TV Producer Attorney
Literacy Coach
Payment Processor
Secretary
Company Manager
Teacher   Personal Assistant
Film & TV Producer
Avionics Engineer
Graduate Student Affairs Officer
Airline Pilot
Registered Nurse   Accountant
Freelance Illustrator
Union Electrician
Acupuncture Therapist
Business Manager   Manager
City Attorney Hearing Officer
Information Technology Manager
Fire & Paramedic Captain
Sales Director
Recruitment Coordinator
Legal Staffing Recruiter
Financial Aid & Public Relations Administrator
Marketing & Promotions Director
Film Editor
Traffic Supervisor
Community Relations Manager
Company President
Customer Service Supervisor

SELF-IDENTIFIED ETHNICITY

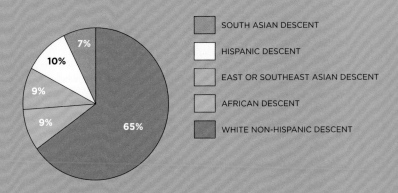

- SOUTH ASIAN DESCENT
- HISPANIC DESCENT
- EAST OR SOUTHEAST ASIAN DESCENT
- AFRICAN DESCENT
- WHITE NON-HISPANIC DESCENT

HOUSEHOLD INCOME: TWO PARENTS COMBINED

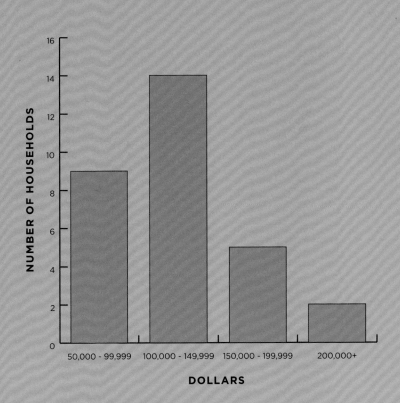

02 Material Saturation: Mountains of Possessions

IF EVERYDAY LIFE in the first few years of the twenty-first century has been characterized by anything, it is the American family's willingness to both work hard and shop hard, purchasing one attractive, well-marketed new product after another and taking on debt in a vigorous show of consumerism. As was also true during the preceding decade or two, this has been a period of materialism at its loftiest, embraced by a wide spectrum of working-class and middle-class families.

And why not? The ability to acquire untold numbers of objects has expanded from the wealthy and upper middle class to families in virtually every socioeconomic bracket, including many below the poverty line. Goods cost us far less in adjusted dollars than ever before, and Americans can choose from hundreds of different models of everything from shampoos and cell phones to flat-screen televisions. Hardworking parents reward themselves with new clothes, electronics, and cars on a regular basis and keep their children happy with the latest Barbies, toys, video games, Pixar/Disney paraphernalia, and brand-name jeans and sneakers. Rafts of consumer statistics from the 1990s and 2000s document staggering profits reaped by manufacturers and retailers.

Sustained material affluence depletes the family paychecks, of course, but it also has significant underlying costs. After a few short years many families amass more than their houses can hold. For these households, closets and garages overflow, and clutter increasingly invades the main living spaces of the home. Our project colleagues recently demonstrated that the Los Angeles parents experience real psychological stress associated with clutter and disarray, not to mention financial anxiety as they get in over their heads with mounting credit card debt.

To close observers of the human condition, the first few years of the twenty-first century in the U.S. represent an unparalleled opportunity to study the tangible artifacts of family life. It is no exaggeration to say that this is the most materially rich society in global history, with light-years more possessions per average family than any preceding society. While elites and royalty of earlier eras often lived amid great affluence at stunningly furnished palaces—Versailles comes to mind—the average European household of the time was sparsely appointed. Even the relative excesses of domestic property that were common during the Victorian period, when it was fashionable to add rugs, mirrors, paintings, and overstuffed chairs to crowded parlors, truly pale by comparison to the total possessions of average families today in the U.S.

These decades of sustained consumer frenzy must have played out in measurable and interesting ways within people's homes, since the home is the storehouse for nearly everything families possess. But the systematic documentation of all the assemblages of goods burdening ordinary, lived-in homes has never been done in the U.S. or any other modern industrial society.

Since people universally treasure their privacy, and a large-scale project like this one is very costly, it has been more or less prohibitive to carry out—until now. We have assembled a record of busy

Los Angeles–area families going about their daily lives amid all of their household things. In this chapter we feature images of vibrant U.S. consumerism and its real and striking impacts at home. We see families' daily struggles with clutter and disarray. Many households grapple with a clutter crisis resulting from the sheer numbers of artifacts they own and try to manage. Clothes, dolls, and boxes overflow closets; food is stockpiled in garages and pantries; toys and media gadgets are everywhere. One family uses a spare shower stall for the dirty laundry. Three-fourths of the families in our study use their garages exclusively for storage and have permanently banished their cars to adjoining driveways and streets.

Still, a skeptic might ask, is American family life unique? Is the U.S. really so different from the rest of the world? The answer is yes, at least in some key respects. Just consider that while American children constitute a tiny fraction of the world's population of children, U.S.

buyers are responsible for annually purchasing a mind-boggling 40 percent of the world's toys (detailed later in this chapter). Accompanying images from the L.A. homes, we assemble important, occasionally staggering data from economic reports and sales or manufacturing figures and track the in-home numbers and spatial distributions of many types of household artifacts.

THE MATERIAL WORLD IN AMERICAN HOMES

Because so many objects are present in the typical family home, enumerating those at all 32 L.A. houses has been a colossal task, cumulatively consuming several thousand hours. Trained coders assigned every photographed object to an overarching category (such as furniture, media electronic, decorative item, or toy) and then directly counted (for most categories) or estimated (for abundant items such as books, CDs, or toys) the numbers of such

items present, room by room. These counts are essential because they provide firm quantitative evidence of the material richness and diversity in modern American homes. Nothing as comprehensive as this archive exists for any other modern culture.

The first household assemblage we analyzed, of Family 27, resulted in a tally of 2,260 visible possessions in the first three rooms coded (two bedrooms and the living room). To be counted, an object must be in plain sight on a table, shelf, wall, floor, closet hanger, etc.; tallies do not include untold numbers of items tucked into dresser drawers, boxes, and cabinets or items positioned behind other items. So the counts we derive are quite conservative figures compared to actual objects owned. Apparel, for instance, simply cannot be counted accurately since most is in closed dressers or cabinets and squeezed into largely hidden closet space.

Family 27 has these thousands of possessions in only a portion of their modest-sized (980 square feet) house's rooms, and they are not at all unique in our study. Small wonder that quite a few of the sampled L.A. houses, which average 1,750 square feet of living space, feel overstuffed and cluttered. Images throughout this chapter reveal many a bedroom, home office, or garage so crammed with objects that it is a challenge for household members to comfortably traverse the space (and for us to arrive at reliable counts).

The words of the parents themselves speak volumes about the effects of clutter and high densities of objects in their homes. Many find their accumulated possessions exhausting to contemplate, organize, and clean. The visual busyness of hoards of objects can affect basic enjoyment of the home. An eye-opening analysis of the households in our study by CELF psychologists Darby Saxbe and Rena Repetti shows that clutter is more than just an annoyance in the house. Mothers

who use key words in their self-narrated home tours indicating that the home is messy or cluttered actually experience a higher rate of depressed mood toward evening, based on cortisol measures over a number of days.

So for the first time, we can link measurably high densities of household objects—what we call "stressful" house environments—with physiological responses that can markedly compromise homeowner health. That is, conspicuous consumption and constant clutter (as defined and experienced by the residents themselves) may be affecting some mothers' long-term well-being. Cortisol data indicate that fathers are relatively unaffected by mess. As one mother videotaped and narrated the home tour of her office/garage area, the frustration in her voice was evident:

> This is the office. It's a total mess. We probably should, you know, organize it better. Here is where the computers are and the kids do homework. We are all on the computers here from time to time.... And here we have the garage, with everything. This is usually a total mess and it's a total mess today again. This is where we have bikes and all the old furniture, sofas, and things that we don't use. It's, how can I say it, it's a mess. It's not fun. It should be cleaned up and we should probably get rid of a whole bunch of stuff. (Mother, Family 6)

Clutter and the aggravation that accompanies it have spurred a robust home-organizing industry, focused especially on closet systems and garage overhauls. Few families in our study have invested in these strategies, however, and most seemed resigned to endless kid-related clutter. Given the astonishing numbers of toys purchased by American families, it is little surprise that children's stuff so thoroughly pervades the main living areas of most houses, from piles of toys on the living room floor to stacks of kids' paraphernalia on dining room tables, kitchen counters, and couches.

Beyond that, it is not unusual to also find kids' art and Disney-themed images in public rooms of homes, giving them a very child-centered look that would have been rare during the middle decades of the twentieth century, when there was far more emphasis on presentation and formality in the living room, dining room, and even kitchen areas.

The core of the kitchen is another visually busy place. The typical U.S. family places quite a few objects on the front panels of the kitchen refrigerator, mostly magnets, snapshots of family and pets, phone numbers, memos, calendars, kids' art, bills, and menus. Angelinos post a lot of decorative magnets, unframed family snapshots from informal moments of family history, and paperwork such as schedules, reminders, and invitations. A few refrigerator "displays" in our study are spare and neat, and several are busy but organized by object type, with, for instance, magnets or photos in neat rows. But most families have rather dense and layered assemblages of ephemera on the refrigerator.

One of the more intriguing phenomena we have noted is a tendency for high counts of objects on refrigerator panels to co-occur with large numbers of objects per square foot *in the house as a whole*. Put another way, a family's tolerance for a "messy" refrigerator may be associated with a fairly relaxed attitude about high density or clutter in public rooms of the house—the living room, family room, dining room, and office. In the small slice of life we have documented in L.A., exceptional densities of household goods, marked clutter, and visually packed refrigerator displays of snapshots, menus, and schedules often go hand-in-hand. Perhaps a place as seemingly unassuming as the refrigerator signals overall family tendencies regarding consumerism and household organization.

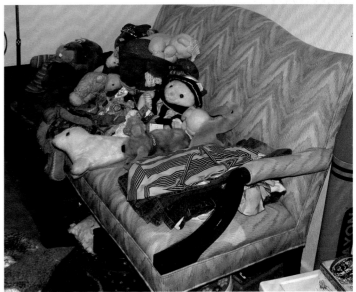

MOST POSSESSIONS PER FAMILY IN GLOBAL HISTORY

For more than 40,000 years, intellectually modern humans have peopled the planet, but never before has any society accumulated so many personal possessions. U.S. households spend on average tens of thousands of dollars every year on new purchases. A substantial portion of these expenditures goes toward replacement goods such as trendy apparel and the latest media electronics, not to mention the newest models of cars. Many of these objects replace perfectly good antecedents that homeowners may only reluctantly part with. The result is typically clutter amassing in "back stage" storage areas such as garages, closets, and attics, eventually extending to "front stage" living spaces. Here we illustrate only a small portion of the possessions that the 32 Los Angeles families have accumulated in their homes.

AVERAGE ANNUAL RETAIL SALES IN U.S. (MID–2000s)

$20.9 billion	The amount received by the nation's retailers for book sales
$11.8 billion	The retail value of 746 million music CDs sold
$24 billion	The cumulative amount paid by shoppers for toys, dolls, and board games
$16 billion	The cost to consumers for 1.2 billion DVDs and VHS tapes
$264.4 billion	The amount consumers paid for 16.5 billion pieces of apparel
$42 billion	The price paid by shoppers for 2 billion pairs of shoes

AVERAGE COUNTS PER LOS ANGELES FAMILY*

Books & Magazines	438
Music CDs	212
Toys	139
DVDs & VHS Tapes	90
Shoes (pairs)	39

Visible artifacts

BARBIE TAKES OVER THE GLOBE

Bevies of Barbies, Beanie Babies, and other dolls preside over the bedrooms of many of the children in the study. These and other consumer icons have taken a huge toll on the budgets of American families for the last few decades. Several of the L.A. households have more than 250 visible dolls, plush toys, action figures, and other toys, and most have at least 100. Untold numbers of others are tucked in closets and under beds.

- **Over one billion** Barbie® dolls have been sold since 1959 in more than 150 countries.

- Mattel sells over **1.5 million dolls each week**, which is equivalent to 215,286 dolls per day and 2.5 dolls per second, or 78,579,390 dolls per year worldwide.

- Barbie doll manufacturing is currently a **$2.5 billion dollar-per-year industry**.

- Clothes made for Barbie and friends have consumed more than **105 million yards of fabric**, making Mattel one of the world's largest apparel manufacturers.

- If all Barbies and kin sold since 1959 were lined up head-to-toe, they would circle the planet **more than seven times**.

> It's pretty cool in my room. I like all the toys... and those are my Barbies. You can sleep, you can read, you can braid doll hair, you can change Barbie clothes. There's all kinds of things: globes, teddy bears, stuffed animals, Barbies, baby dolls, tea sets, games, a piano, melody harp, a guitar, tea sets, more baby clothes, cassettes, Barbie school, doctor kits...
>
> **Daughter (Age 8), Family 27**

THE ENUMERATION OF DOLLS*

Beanie Babies	165
Human/Animal Figurines	36
Barbie Dolls	22
Other Dolls	20
Porcelain Dolls	3
Troll	1
Castle Miniature	1

Display shelf, girl's bedroom, Family 1 (pictured left)

> " Ah, there are all the Beanie Babies. Look how beautiful they are. Do you have a favorite one? I just want to show all those Barbies. Okay, there's Ken, oh that's Elvis…
>
> **Mother (Age 48), Family 1**

> Every good girl should have a whole ton of Barbies...
>
> **Mother (Age 41), Family 27**

CHILD-CENTERED HOMES

The United States has 3.1 percent of the world's children, yet U.S. families annually purchase more than 40 percent of the total toys consumed globally. Spilling out of children's bedrooms and into living rooms, dining rooms, kitchens, and parents' bedrooms, the playthings of America's kids are ubiquitous in middle-class homes. In the mid-2000s, U.S. consumers were spending more than $240 annually per child on toys alone.

A sense among working parents that they have less time to spend with their children may be spurring them to shower kids with toys to compensate for a perceived loss of quality time at home. Other relatives contribute to children's material assemblages, including about $500 spent by grandparents each year on toys, clothes, books, and other gifts. Given the high divorce rate in the U.S., many children wind up getting gifts from multiple sets of grandparents.

Our data suggest that each new child in a household leads to a 30 percent increase in a family's inventory of possessions during the preschool years alone. Masses of toys and kids' gear inevitably spread throughout the house, and some parents allow—and even feature—Disney-inspired art and collectibles reflecting children's themes in traditionally adult spaces such as living rooms.

AVERAGE ANNUAL RETAIL TOY SALES IN U.S. (MID-2000s)

$3.1 billion	Infant & Preschool Toys
$2.7 billion	Dolls
$2.7 billion	Outdoor & Sports Toys
$2.4 billion	Arts & Crafts
$2.4 billion	Games & Puzzles
$1.8 billion	Toy Vehicles
$1.3 billion	Action Figures
$1.3 billion	Plush Toys
$0.7 billion	Building Sets
$0.4 billion	Educational Toys

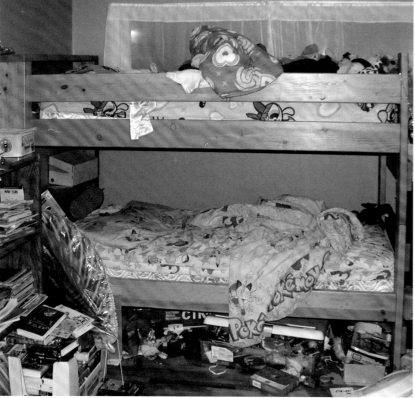

MESS AND STRESS

Middle-class families purchase mountains of toys, clothes, and other goods marketed for children, much of which accumulates in crowded bedrooms with floor surfaces that rarely see the light of day. Parents' own words speak to the stress that comes with not having the time to attend to the material aftermath of kids' activities.

> Now the kids' room has a lot going on in it. We have a bunk bed because of our issues with space. The closet is extremely unutilized because we usually can't get to it.
>
> **Father (Age 33), Family 5**

> Five people living in a small house. There is a lot of stuff and a lot of clothes. And we do not have enough closet space for everything. It's a mess. It's not fun.
>
> **Mother (Age 45), Family 6**

Busy two-income families are challenged to find time to organize and create order in cramped bedrooms and home offices littered with paper, clothes, and files. More than half of the households in the study have home office spaces for work and schoolwork. We find many kinds of artifacts in these spaces beyond the expected documents, computers, and desks. Indeed, home offices attract miscellaneous objects that fit poorly elsewhere, resulting in clutter that parents find stressful. Not including abundant stacks of papers, mail, and magazines, which we deemed impossible to tally with accuracy, the viewable artifact total is 372 in the heavily used home office pictured above. In other home offices, our coding project documented as few as 21 and as many as 2,337 plainly visible non-paper objects.

> " This is very chaotic.
>
> **Mother (Age 40), Family 29**

> This is the mess I see when I walk into my house. Probably five, six times a day I am cleaning up...
>
> **Mother (Age 45), Family 6**

THE GARAGE: CARS OUT, EVERYTHING ELSE IN

Cars have been banished from 75 percent of garages to make way for rejected furniture and cascading bins and boxes of mostly forgotten household goods. Our analysis suggests that close to 90 percent of garage square footage in middle-class L.A. neighborhoods may now be used for storage rather than automobiles.

The Family 16 garage (opposite) yielded a count of 511 visible objects on the day it was photographed. More telling, we documented nearly 65 different categories of artifacts in this space. Archaeological analyses from a wide array of cultural contexts indicate that counts alone tell us how much stuff a household possesses, but counts combined with object diversity in material assemblages can tell a nuanced behavioral story. High diversity indices in this garage and other L.A. garage assemblages suggest that artifacts are coming from many discrete areas of the house interior, and they are coming from multiple family members. We frequently observe foods, art, clothing, shoes, furniture, books, records, document files, seasonal items, and stockpiles of paper products.

U.S. families have trouble getting rid of their possessions, even those they box up and move to liminal spaces such as garages and basements. Whether they cannot break sentimental attachments to certain objects, do not have the time to sort through and make decisions, or believe objects have value and could be sold on eBay, most families struggle to cope with stored clutter. Beyond what they keep at home, figures from 2005 show that 1 in 11 U.S. households rents offsite storage for additional belongings, occupying an astonishing 1.875 billion square feet of real estate. These high nationwide figures make it clear that the cramped-house syndrome is not just a California phenomenon and is not attributable solely to the absence of basements. Many easterners, southerners, and midwesterners have also outgrown their attic, garage, and basement spaces and moved their surpluses into overflow spaces provided by the booming domestic storage industry.

Although several of the garages in the study are tidy and contain as few as 50 countable objects, the typical chaotic garage bursts at the seams with 300-650 boxes, plastic storage bins, and many spillover items from inside the house. These items actually predominate at most homes over traditional garage artifacts such as mowers, tools, car items, bikes, lumber, and sports gear. Actual counts of possessions in garages are far higher, perhaps two to three times the numbers we have, but many objects are hidden underneath or behind others and cannot be counted.

REFRIGERATORS: SNAPSHOTS OF FAMILY LIFE

The typical L.A. refrigerator front panel (in some cases also a side panel) is host to a mean of 52 objects, which consume up to 90 percent of the surface space. Decorative magnets are the most common objects on refrigerators, many of them mementos of places such as cities and national parks, reminding the family of past travels. A common subcategory is the advertisement magnet from the local plumber or the insurance company, ensuring that useful phone numbers are posted in a highly visible place. Doing double duty securing other objects, magnets provide a way to display informal family snapshots as well as school menus, kids' art, and calendars. The family with the most extensive refrigerator display has more than 125 magnets and 9 family photos among the 166 objects vying for space. Some refrigerators are nearly free of these items, but most have high object densities and are visually busy. The two refrigerators at right are typical of the high-density examples.

WHAT'S ON REFRIGERATORS?

FAMILY 1 (OPPOSITE LEFT)

Magnets	52
Photographs	35
Magnetic Photo Frames	6
Child's Art Projects	1
Schedules	1
Postcards	1
Achievement/Awards	1
Total Artifacts	97

FAMILY 19 (OPPOSITE RIGHT)

Magnets	46
Photographs	2
Magnetic Photo Frames	2
Child's Art Projects	6
Child's Schoolwork	1
Calendars	12
Lists	1
Schedules	1
Coupons	2
Invitations	1
Rosters	1
White Boards	1
Charts	1
Take-out Menus	1
Total Artifacts	78

> And then of course there's the refrigerator. And I don't know what American couple has a refrigerator that doesn't get things stuck to it. You can see that there's quite a lot of things stuck to ours. Pictures, reminders, addresses, phone lists that have not been good for years and years.

Mother (Age 41), Family 27

REFRIGERATOR DISPLAYS: A LINK TO HOUSEHOLD CONSUMPTION

As the sample of L.A. households expanded during our several years of fieldwork, we noticed an interesting pattern: the numbers of objects families place on their refrigerators appear to signal something about the possessions they have in the rest of the house. Specifically, the look of the refrigerator door hints at the sheer quantities of possessions a family has and how they are organized or arranged in the home. By organization we mean the visual impact, which is a function of both the density and the neatness of the distribution of objects. A simple analysis using our coded material culture inventories reveals that a family's tolerance for a crowded, artifact-laden refrigerator surface often corresponds to the densities of possessions in the main rooms of the house (living/family room, dining room, office, kitchen).

We grouped the six households with the highest refrigerator display counts (all with at least 80 artifacts) and the seven households with the lowest counts (all with fewer than 20), then aggregated the artifact counts from the main rooms of each house. Houses in the first group yield a mean of 1,448 visible objects in the main rooms, whereas families in the second group, with their tidy and minimally decorated refrigerators, tend to have only modest assemblages of objects (a mean of 322) visible in the home, a striking difference. The other 19 households reflect neither extreme, as would be expected.

The two sets of counts alone do not reveal a statistically significant correlation, but we think it also necessary to factor in several other variables, such as how long families have occupied their houses and when they last did a major "spring" cleaning. Most important of all, we must arrive at a way to best measure the complex conditions that we label "tidiness" and "clutter." Sheer numbers are just a part of the whole—these terms encompass equal parts the numbers of items present, how they are organized, and whether they are out of place. Quantification is a challenge: psychologists studying people who accumulate extreme quantities of material goods, quantum leaps beyond any of the households in this study, have struggled for years with just how to define with precision the varying degrees of clutter in homes.

Still, what we observed thus far is of considerable interest to scholars of modern material culture. This iconic place in the American home—the refrigerator panel—may function as a measuring stick for how intensively families are participating in consumer purchasing and how many household goods they retain over their lifetimes.

> " Here is our life on the refrigerator and all of the collection of photos and magnets. And you know what? We do go up to these pictures all the time and sort of remark about who people are and where we were and what we were doing and how old people were.
>
> **Father (Age 41), Family 1**

03 Food, Food, Food

FOOD PLAYS multiple, pivotal, and conflicting roles in American life. Much more so than in other cultures, we tend to schedule our meals to fit in like necessary appointments amid a blizzard of daily activities. Yet we embrace our favorite foods to excess, and tens of millions of Americans have become alarmingly overweight. Some $12 billion in advertising dollars is spent annually to persuade Americans to buy new foods or to patronize restaurants, particularly fast-food restaurants.

According to the USDA, food marketing is the nation's second largest advertiser, surpassed only by the auto industry. The foods featured in ads are overwhelmingly of the packaged variety, including breakfast cereals, candy, beer, soft drinks, snacks, nuts, and coffee. Paltry amounts by comparison are spent on promoting the consumption of fruits and other fresh foods. Corporations introduce 10,000 new processed food products every year in the U.S. Despite knowing better, many Americans harbor unhealthy ideas about what and how much to eat.

When we sharpen our lens to examine the daily dining habits of specific families in Los Angeles, the picture is more complex. It is clear that some parents devote time and energy to healthy approaches to mealtimes. They prepare dinners using at least a few fresh and unprocessed ingredients, and they spend a few more minutes, on average, completing the cooking. Several others parents say they would do better if only they could squeeze it into their schedules. They cite the limited time they have available after work to plan and make a nice homemade meal. Some families routinely lean more heavily on carry-out, frozen foods, and pre-packaged foods. All told, we find that families that cook fresh foods with regularity are in the minority.

Our observations pertaining to food encompass digitized film and photos of about 90 dinners, a similar number of breakfasts, and the foods stored at home in refrigerators, freezers, cupboards, and elsewhere. Beyond the meal-preparation practices and the foods served and consumed by families, we also document moment-by-moment family interactions and togetherness at mealtimes. In stark contrast to practices of many cultures around the world, American families appear to place only a modest premium on the importance of dining together, defined as eating at the same time and while in the same room. While this is true, we find in actuality a wide range of variation and many complexities in families' co-dining practices.

U.S. families also exhibit a strong propensity to stockpile food. Mega-packages of drinks, soups, canned vegetables, meats, ice cream, and related goods (paper towels, tissues, pet food, etc.) acquired from "big-box" stores overflow into second refrigerators, extra freezers, and garages. With their long shelf lives and bulk-rate prices, such goods provide flexibility and convenience. Fresh fruits and vegetables do not stockpile well and inconveniently go bad if a family is too time-stressed to prepare a fresh meal during the harried work week. Perhaps it should be no surprise that fresh foods occupy smaller portions of the diet than in decades past.

Each day, one in four American adults goes to a fast-food restaurant.

PREDICTABILITY

American families seem to relish the predictability of pre-packaged foods—one knows exactly how long it will take to make a meal and how it will taste. George Ritzer contends that this is one of the byproducts of the "McDonaldization" of America. During the 1950s, the U.S. fast-food enterprise, led by McDonald's, introduced standardized portion sizes, unvarying ingredients, and universal preparation processes while lowering cost through mass-production of moderate-quality foods. According to *Fast Food Nation* author Eric Schlosser, these same concepts wound their way into our kitchens during the 1960s and 1970s and never left.

Near-perfect predictability in the form of processed and frozen ingredients or entrees allows dinner preparation to be knocked down a few pegs and liberated to take its place in the multi-tasking milieu that characterizes the working mother's (or father's) work week. Meal preparation simply has to be slotted in alongside other late afternoon activities such as helping the kids with homework, chatting on the phone, doing laundry, paying bills, or catching the news on TV.

Among American families, the now-entrenched impacts of fast-food culture on mealtime dynamics are evident in a general eagerness to save time—more so than cost—and reduce complexity during meal preparation. In our Los Angeles study, on average about 25 percent of evening meals involve no home labor: the food is obtained via carry-out, delivery, or at a restaurant with friends and family.

For the remainder of their dinners, these families purchase and eat a remarkable array of foods. Quite often family dinners rely wholly on frozen, canned, or boxed convenience items. The most popular strategy is the use of fresh ingredients in conjunction with prepared (canned or boxed) products such as flavored rice or canned soups. Just one in four meals is home-cooked from scratch. Altogether, the weeknight dinners that our Los Angeles families produced at home were prepared with processed, commercial foods about two-thirds of the time.

THE MYTH OF "CONVENIENCE" FOODS

Observations from the Los Angeles families show that the thousands of new processed foods brought on the market each year—commonly called convenience foods—do not on average get the family dinner ready to devour notably faster than cooked-from-scratch entrees. Considering all cases in our sample, the average dinner takes 52 minutes to get on the table, start to finish, including microwave or oven time. When families use mostly convenience foods for the meal, they wind up saving a bit under 5 minutes total (a statistically insignificant figure).

Mom or Dad spends, on average, about the same number of minutes preparing a simple made-from-scratch meal on Monday and a multi-option dinner (two or more courses or choices) of solely pre-packaged items on Tuesday. The slicing and dicing already done at a food-production facility slightly reduces hands-on work for the Tuesday dinner.

Perhaps the most important and clear-cut effect of packaged foods is that they reduce the complexity of meal planning. Dinners centered on convenience foods require less shopping time and planning time since many separate ingredients do not have to be assembled. The family chef can invest less time thinking about the week's meals.

> So yeah a lot of stuff is pre-packaged, which I just warm up. Like for breakfast, Hot Pockets pastries. They also have Hot Pockets pizza, stuff like that, things that I can just microwave. Pizza, chicken pot pies. These are more like emergency food or easy, easy things to make... So I have a combination of stuff that we prepare ourselves or things that are already pre-packaged that you just throw in the microwave or the oven.
>
> **Mother (Age 42), Family 23**

WEEKDAY DINNERS: Families in the study make about one-quarter of their weekday dinners from scratch with fresh ingredients—using few or no convenience foods. When we isolate and measure just the "hands-on" preparation time required (for opening, peeling, chopping, stirring), our CELF colleague Margaret Beck finds that cooking from scratch adds only 10 to 12 minutes compared to the hands-on time needed to prepare a convenience-food meal.

Moms in the Los Angeles study are the sole preparers of weekday dinners 60 percent of the time and are notably involved in cooking dinners 93 percent of the time.

Dads are the sole preparers of weekday dinners 7 percent of the time and are involved in some way in 33 percent of preparations. The statistically significant differences in parents' contributions to dinner preparation echo gender-based disparities in other spheres of household work among the Los Angeles families. Mothers still invest more time in household tasks, as many reports confirm has been true in the broader U.S. for decades. But our data show that L.A. fathers on average work at jobs for longer hours and spend more time commuting than the mothers. As such, fathers are usually the last to arrive home.

AVERAGE "HANDS-ON" DINNER PREPARATION TIME

COOKING FROM SCRATCH
38 MINUTES

USING PRE-PACKAGED FOODS
26 MINUTES

"HOME-COOKED" DINNERS FROM THE FREEZER

Time is the scarce resource that seems to drive food purchasing and cooking strategies among Los Angeles families. From baby boomers to younger parents who started families in the 1980s and 1990s, today's U.S. food buyers grew up with frozen convenience foods and share the view that using them saves substantial time and effort. The great proliferation of frozen commercial foods is matched only by our eagerness to consume them.

But our perceptions about the minutes spent on household tasks are not always accurate. Margaret Beck's analysis of the L.A. families shows that cooking with frozen food as a major component in the dinner takes less hands-on preparation time, but the total elapsed time to prepare the full meal is barely shortened compared to cooking from scratch. Thus the real difference is the effort needed at the planning stages.

Frozen foods require less advance planning and less cooking knowledge and skills than acquiring and working with raw ingredients to assemble

a dinner. Busy, fully employed mothers (and one-third of fathers who do some cooking) may have little time to pick up culinary skills.

Grocery consultants and the American Frozen Food Institute report that the average length of the frozen food aisles in grocery stores is a whopping 400 linear feet, double what it was in 1990. Americans purchase far more varieties of frozen and packaged foods than ever before.

> " The freezer is full of stuff. Extra things that are on sale. Go-Gurts and butter and chicken and ice cream. Extra meat. I think there's a whole ham back there because Ralphs gave us a free ham one time, and it's in there. And just different things... cheeses and ice cream. Stuff. Extra stuff.
>
> **Mother (Age 41), Family 16**

The Federal Trade Commission estimates that food and beverage companies invest $1.6 billion annually convincing children to eat unhealthy food. During the past 30 years, obesity rates have tripled among U.S. teens. One-third of children are now overweight or obese. These children are far more likely than peers to have high blood pressure, high cholesterol, and Type II diabetes.

What we call "home-cooked meals" are those dinners prepared *in the home* using pre-packaged, frozen, or fresh foods, or combinations of these with take-out foods. Other categories of evening meals are eating at relatives' homes, dining at restaurants, and eating take-out at home.

MEAL SOURCES: THE LOS ANGELES FAMILIES

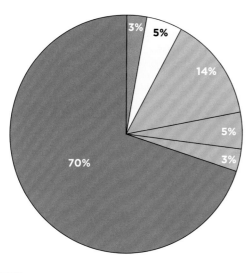

- HOME-COOKED FOR EVERYONE
- GUESTS AT GRANDPARENTS
- RESTAURANT
- TAKE-OUT
- HOME-COOKED/TAKE-OUT
- HOME-COOKED FOR CHILDREN ONLY

L.A. parents associate home-cooked meals with "being healthy" and "eating well."

> " You get into saving time, cutting corners, not having enough money to buy the ideal foods. I think that today we're just so much more aware of what we should be eating.
>
> **Mother (Age 37), Family 5**

> " Yeah, we eat a lot of fresh vegetables and fruits, too. Well, I should say, we have them on hand. ((laughs)) We do try to eat them.
>
> **Mother (Age 41), Family 16**

> " This is my favorite pasta sauce—Walnut Acres Tomato Basil. Whole Foods or Pavilions carries it in the organic section. It's very good. I don't have time to make my own sauce, although I have in the past.
>
> **Mother (Age 50), Family 14**

FAMILIES: EATING DINNER TOGETHER?

	U.S. FAMILIES: SELF-REPORTED	LOS ANGELES FAMILIES: FILMED

ALWAYS	50%	17%
USUALLY	34%	60%
NEVER	16%	23%

DINING TOGETHER

Half of U.S. families report that they eat dinner together every day, and another 34 percent say they eat together much of the time, according to a recent *USA Today* survey. Although these numbers seem low and contrast starkly with traditional ideals of family togetherness, unity, and communication, they may actually exaggerate the degree to which families eat dinners in the same room and at the same time.

Our film and observations of more than 90 family dinnertimes indicate that just one in six (17 percent) of the L.A. families consistently eat dinner together, a figure significantly lower than what American families self report. Nearly one-quarter of the families did not dine together at all during the study. Even when all family members are at home, they gather to consume the evening meal together just 60 percent of the time.

U.S. families experience many fragmented evening meals due to the challenging pace and schedule of the typical work week. The flexibility afforded by packaged foods facilitates fragmented dinners.

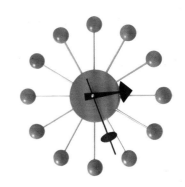

DINNERS BY THE MINUTE

The duration of typical American dinners pales by comparison to primary meals in many parts of Europe, where people still savor the quality of foods and relish the social interactions enjoyed during a good meal. On weeknights in the Los Angeles study, the average duration of the dinners is 29.5 minutes. On weekends, dinners last 33.2 minutes.

The limited minutes families spend eating are often entangled with other facets of life. Unrelated activities happen during one-third of dinners in our sample, usually centered on homework, television, or phone calls. As well, kitchen tabletops and even formal dining room tables in some homes are left fully laden with piles of bills, bulky toys, and the ephemera of daily living while diners are eating.

Further evidence for the declining importance U.S. families attach to eating together—or the difficulty they have making it happen—is captured by our scan sampling method; we tracked many comings and goings of various family members during mealtimes. What we call "fragmented" dinners, those in which family members eat sequentially or in different rooms, are commonplace for nearly two-thirds of the study households. All told, 41 percent of the 90 dinners we observed were fragmented.

Children often start the cascade of staggered eating by pleading to eat different packaged foods when they do not like the main dish. Contestations over what to eat often result in different main dishes for children that may not be ready at the same time as what parents eat. Busy schedules also intrude. Meals are eaten when and where children and the non-cooking parent find it convenient, sometimes near TVs in the living room or bedroom.

U.S. parents focus on nutritional qualities of food—the vitamins and proteins—and the link between food consumption and health, while Italians focus on the pleasures of eating food.

STOCKPILING

Beyond the ice cream, frozen vegetables, and meats that traditionally occupy freezer space, American freezers today overflow with both individual-sized and mega-sized packaged foods. Entrees from regional cuisines (Indian, Mexican, Thai, Italian, Korean, Chinese, and more) are side-by-side with the more generic "American" foods: chicken strips, waffles, frozen yogurt bars, pizza, fish sticks, pockets, wraps, wings, nuggets, and hot dogs, to note a few. These microwavable convenience foods contribute to the frequency with which children opt out at dinnertime by begging to eat something other than what parents have prepared.

Close to half (47 percent) of the Los Angeles families keep second refrigerator/freezers, almost always in the garage. The common overflow foods in the second refrigerator are beer, water, soft drinks, and frozen foods. Nine percent of households actually have a third one, usually a mini-refrigerator.

> Freezer... freezer is the bane of Jerry's existence. He hates it, cause it's so full. He can't make ice because there are chicken nuggets in it.
>
> **Mother (Age 41), Family 16**

> Here in the garage we keep water, Gatorade, cereals, pretzel packs...
>
> **Mother (Age 37), Family 5**

Stockpiling is an efficient foraging strategy for parents who want to minimize the number of times they have to round up young children and get them in and out of car seats and shopping carts. Big grocery trips slated for weekends also help to circumvent some of the stress of shopping with hungry kids during busy weekday afternoons, when family schedules are already full with dinner preparations, homework, baths, and next-day planning.

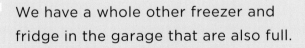

" We have a whole other freezer and fridge in the garage that are also full.

Mother (Age 41), Family 16

Big-box stores reward stockpiling by consumers because their parent corporations maximize profits through bulk selling. Efficiencies in labor expended on packaging and handling reduce costs that can be passed along to shoppers eager for bargains.

> " We're a Costco family. I should just buy stock.
>
> **Mother (age 42), Family 23**

04 Vanishing Leisure

LEISURE IS AN important aspect of individual and family life in all cultures. Social scientists studying modern industrial societies typically focus on the hours devoted to jobs and the time spent on entertainment and other leisure activities away from the home. Far less scrutiny is applied to the leisure time people experience when behind closed doors at their residences. These activities can be self-reported with some reliability, but because they occur out of the public eye, it has not been feasible to systematically film and time what parents and kids really do (rather than what they think they do, or think they ought to report). This chapter is about where and how often families carve out time for relaxing activities—that is, when they are not working, caretaking, or doing household tasks.

Americans spend considerable sums of money to create leisure "refuges" such as master bedroom suites (Chapter 7) and back yard patios, both often featuring "spa" tubs. Yet leisure at home— the expectation of free evenings and weekends—is a fairly recent phenomenon in the U.S., arising from growing distinctions during the first half of the 1900s between time spent at jobs and time at home away from work. The car and the explosion of electronic media also have contributed to a long-term decline in collective and interactive leisure and a rise in passive and more private and isolated leisure activities. Time-diary data from across the U.S. in the 1960s–90s document increased television viewing and decreased interaction with others outside the interior home environment.

INDOOR LEISURE

So how much leisure time do busy twenty-first century parents really have when they are at home? In terms of percentage of our systematic scan-sampling observations at the house, the Los Angeles parents are doing leisurely things during just 14 percent of those observations. Moreover, virtually all of their home-based leisure activities take place indoors. Indeed, the parents are rarely outdoors at all, with fully 92 percent of scan-sampling observations (including leisure and non-leisure time) occurring inside the house. This is a striking finding in a city where the mild climate allows for outdoor activity year-round. Such a pronounced indoor orientation is probably greatly magnified in the colder regions of the U.S.

For parents, TV watching (including DVD and VCR use) is the most frequent leisure activity, consuming about 50 percent of their limited leisure time, followed by reading a newspaper, book, or magazine (about 21 percent). These largely non-interactive activities together account for over two-thirds of parents' leisure. Parents do spend some time daily (18 percent of leisure time) playing games or doing puzzles, playing in general with their children, or observing family members in various activities. Video games and recreational Internet use round out the list of common leisure activities.

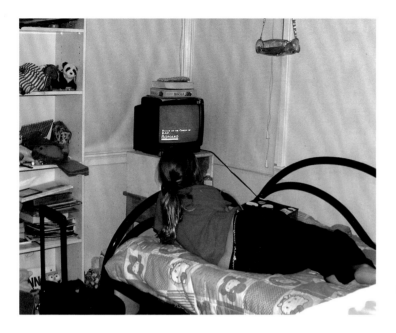

Where do leisure activities occur? Two-thirds of parents' leisure time is spent in the living room/family room spaces, with the TV a common focal point. Parents use the kitchen and dining room for 16 percent of their leisure time, including activities such as reading, being attentive toward family, and television viewing. Parents spend slightly less of their leisure time (14 percent) in various bedrooms. Much of this time is spent watching TV and resting. Children's bedrooms often bring parents and children together for short periods centered on games and puzzles, recreational Internet use, and shared reading. Almost none of parents' leisure takes place in home offices or outside.

The Los Angeles mothers and fathers rarely experience the luxury of extended bouts of leisure. Instead, they have highly fragmented leisure episodes—brief periods of relaxation repeatedly interrupted by other needs, such as attending to a child. The average duration of parents' leisure episodes is between 10 and 20 minutes. Fathers tend to enjoy more and lengthier leisure periods than mothers overall—although this is not true for all families. Within families where the gender gap in leisure time is quite pronounced in the father's favor, their spouses are frustrated by the disparity. Several of the mothers in the L.A. study who see themselves in this situation do not hesitate to express dissatisfaction with chronic imbalances of free time. They talk about it in their home tours, in interviews we conducted, and occasionally in daily interactions with the family.

Parents also lament leisure activities that they no longer pursue. Several have given up playing the piano, guitar, or drums for lack of time. A large-scale 2000 survey of U.S. parents shows that nearly 60 percent

of married fathers and more than 70 percent of mothers assert that they have too little time for themselves. One father in our study says, "I try to go to sleep late or wake up early... so I can have space and time for myself to do whatever." Our scan-sampling data reveal that some mothers routinely rise early in the morning to carve out a few rare moments of leisure time before others in the house awaken.

Children enjoy quite a bit more leisure time at home than their parents do—40 percent of their hours there are spent in leisure—but they spend much of it indoors, mainly in passive contexts such as TV watching and video-game playing. With school, extracurricular activities, and homework competing for their attention, their weeks are nearly as harried as those of their parents, and few activities draw them out to their back yard spaces. These patterns are not confined to Los Angeles: a recent statistical analysis shows that the Los Angeles time-use results are consistent with a large-scale University of Chicago study of activities at middle-class homes that draws on 500 two-income families from multiple cities across the U.S.

OUTDOOR TIME

More and more, outdoor spaces at home go unused by dual-earner families, although the mere presence of the yard and attractive features surrounding the house may generate a positive response and sense of well-being. But the dissipation of outdoor leisure for most of these families is alarming. Parents in L.A. struggle to find any time to enjoy the furnished, private outdoor spaces they have worked so hard to create.

Leisure includes entertaining, playing games, watching TV, video gaming, exercising, playing with the kids, playing sports, snacking, smoking, drinking, playing with pets, doing crafts, whistling, chatting, mid-day napping, and relaxing.

Back yards are important elements in the operation of the home and its presentation to the world. People today can barely imagine an earlier reality when American urban back yards featured trash dumps, coal ashes, and outhouses, but this was true during the early 1900s. Major shifts in residential design over time, such as the arrangement of rooms within the house and the shape of residential lots, have had significant effects on the ways that back yards and patios were used through the twentieth century. A growing desire for privacy also accounts for changing home configurations.

During the early 1900s, as streets became busier with traffic noise and lights, families largely abandoned socializing on their front porches. They attached growing importance to activities in quiet and private spaces. During the 1920s, terraces and verandas were increasingly placed behind houses, and the back of the house was no longer dominated by activities linked with the kitchen. Garages were moved from the back margins of lots, where they had first functioned as carriage houses or sheds for early cars, to the front when autos became ubiquitous. Indoor plumbing brought bathrooms inside.

The back yard was at last opened for socializing and personal expression. By the mid-1940s, the back yard came into its own as a refuge, an outdoor living room, and a place to show off to friends and neighbors. Homes in emerging suburbs, like the new planned community of Levittown on Long Island, had their white picket fences and back yard entertaining areas, and owning such homes became the American dream. By the 1950s, the role of back yards as essential loci for entertaining, exercise, recreation, and cooking was embedded in the American psyche.

> " I'm a couch potato... on the weekends and whenever I get the opportunity. Yeah, I sit and watch TV, listen to my music, my stereo.
>
> **Father (Age 42), Family 17**

Today, the ideal of serenity and relaxation in "outdoor rooms" after work and on weekends is not being achieved. Busy parents largely admire yards from inside the house. The family home tour narratives

Outdoor leisure remains a strongly expressed ideal but is a fading commodity for families pulled in many directions by the demands of work, school, extracurricular events, and indoor entertainment.

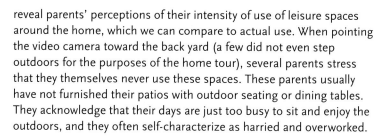

reveal parents' perceptions of their intensity of use of leisure spaces around the home, which we can compare to actual use. When pointing the video camera toward the back yard (a few did not even step outdoors for the purposes of the home tour), several parents stress that they themselves never use these spaces. These parents usually have not furnished their patios with outdoor seating or dining tables. They acknowledge that their days are just too busy to sit and enjoy the outdoors, and they often self-characterize as harried and overworked.

Many parents lament that their nice outdoor spaces are devoid of children's activity as well, commenting that the kids are not using the pool, swing sets, or grassy areas for play anymore. Children's interests increasingly keep them within the home for homework, TV, or computer games, or they are drawn to organized activities away from home.

On the other hand, some families' home tour narratives refer to an intensity of use of outdoor spaces that does not resonate with our direct observations. Both parents in one family assert that they use their back yard and new deck all the time, but no leisure activity by any family member was observed there. This of course could happen in any given period due to extenuating circumstances, but overestimates may also reflect the effects of emotional and financial investments in the space. Parents may want to believe that their real-time use of their back yards is substantial and measures up to half-century-old American cultural norms, but they use these spaces less than families did in earlier decades and far less than they would like.

More than half of the families in the Los Angeles study spent zero leisure time (none for kids, none for parents) in their back yards during our filming. In quite a few of these cases, no family member so much as stepped into the back yard for any purpose. For another 25 percent of the families, the parents did not carve out any back yard leisure (relax,

> Unless I wake up at five o'clock in the morning, you know, I don't really have any spare time, with the kids and my school work. I really wanted to start walking …. I have a treadmill but we don't really have any place here for it.
>
> **Mother (Age 28), Family 8**

> This is our back yard. I'm really never out here. I haven't been out here in a long time.
>
> **Daughter (Age 16), Family 4**

play, eat, read, drink, or swim) despite the presence of pricey features such as built-in pools, spas, above-ground pools, dining sets, lounge chairs, and swing sets. Children in this group of families enjoyed brief periods of outdoor recreation, but less than one hour in each case.

Children used the back yard for more than an hour at only 8 of the 32 L.A. homes. Among the rare instances of sustained leisure for parents, we observed that one or both parents of just three households joined their children in back yard play lasting more than an hour. Outdoor dining is also rare: in all of the weeks of our filming, only three families ate a meal outside together. Not much of the classic "California outdoor living" is happening at these homes.

ACROSS AMERICA the disparity in families' uses of indoor spaces and yard spaces has become much greater in recent years, marking a strong trend toward more sedentary, indoor living. Poorer long-term health among American adult and juvenile populations mirrors this pattern (along with related variables of diet and exercise).

This abandonment of the outdoors is ironic since it was in southern California that architects originally developed classic, mid-century houses with open floor plans, walls of windows, and designs for indoor/outdoor living in private back yard spaces. Residential modernism was rooted in post-war California culture—centering on leisure, the beach, back-yard cookouts, and built-in pools. Images of the hip, sun-splashed homes of celebrities appeared frequently on television and in film. Since families everywhere could view these idealized lifestyles, iconic California designs became influential models for the rest of the U.S.

> "We actually built this house from scratch. We tore down an existing back half of a duplex, and wanted to keep the back yard footprint and still have plenty of room on the inside. We wanted to keep our back yard for a play area, so instead of building a real garage, we built this car-port-like thing. And because of that, we have a bigger back yard, but the problem is, we don't have much storage space.
>
> **Father (Age 40), Family 29**

> "We don't spend time [there]... more because of a lack of time than other things. But what I like about this back yard is that nobody sees us from the street. Ann used to plant tomatoes all year round on this side fence with the neighbors. It was very nice. She hasn't had the time this year to do it, so she's not going to.
>
> **Father (Age 43), Family 27**

Children choose indoor activities for about 90 percent of their leisure time at home, dominated by TV, video games, play with toys and puzzles, and general play with siblings and friends. Much of this play is sedentary and solitary. Outdoor pools, sports equipment, and expansive grassy yards are rarely used. Some families keep blinds and curtains perpetually closed.

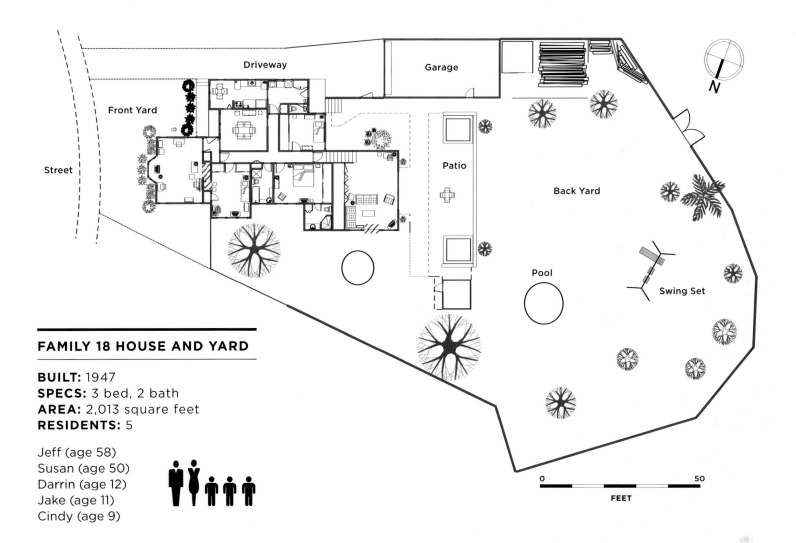

Street

Front Yard

Driveway

Garage

Patio

Back Yard

Pool

Swing Set

N

0   50
FEET

FAMILY 18 HOUSE AND YARD

BUILT: 1947
SPECS: 3 bed, 2 bath
AREA: 2,013 square feet
RESIDENTS: 5

Jeff (age 58)
Susan (age 50)
Darrin (age 12)
Jake (age 11)
Cindy (age 9)

This family's vast back yard (14,850 square feet) went unused during the study. Their home tour narrations confirm that throughout the year, family members only infrequently use their outdoor space. Although they have furnished the yard with a pool, swing set, trampoline, batting cage, patio, and dining table, the parents and children rarely venture out.

LOS ANGELES BACK YARDS

Average size	2,540 sq ft
Size range	600–14,850 sq ft
Average use by parents	< 15 min/week
Average use by children	< 40 min/week

> " We haven't spent a lot of time out in the back, and hopefully, we will soon.
>
> **Mother (Age 38), Family 3**

> " Relaxing time is back here, which seldom ever happens.
>
> **Mother (Age 28), Family 8**

05 Kitchens as Command Centers

THE TERM "COMMAND CENTER" may evoke images of a high-tech room at an intelligence agency, replete with control panels, communications equipment, and mission-focused personnel scurrying among workstations. Such rooms are popular visual backdrops to Hollywood portrayals of NASA's Mission Control in Houston or the headquarters of the FBI.

Kitchens? This analogy hardly applies to the kitchens of most empty nesters or seniors. But the twenty-first century kitchens of working parents with school-age children parallel the model of a command center in several respects. The kitchen is perhaps the most important space in daily family life: a site of frequent congregation, information exchange, collaboration, negotiation, and child socialization. It is a crucial hub of logistical organization and everyday operations for dual-income households.

Kitchens in Los Angeles family homes are typically small, making these spaces seemingly less than desirable for frequent family interaction or diverse activities. Among the 32 houses in our sample, kitchen spaces range from a modest 63 square feet to a roomy 308 square feet. Few of the kitchens have been remodeled by current or previous owners, but those that are updated are bigger and better matched to the exigencies of modern family life.

More than 70 percent of single-family detached houses in the greater Los Angeles region were built prior to 1970. As such, the designs of most homes in our study reflect mid-century perspectives on the family, including the household division of labor featuring the male breadwinner and the female homemaker. Kitchens of the era were viewed as women's spaces, compartmentalized and accessed through closable doors. House designs deliberately excluded kitchens from the flow of the rest of the house.

Key household activities in kitchens encompassed all kinds of domestic backstage work, including cooking, laundry, and other tasks typically performed by women. Interactive family activities were supposed to unfold in dining rooms and living rooms, the more public of residential spaces. One obvious remnant of these 1940s–60s-era designs is the washer-dryer set in the kitchen, often positioned near a service door.

Times have changed, to say the least. While mid-twentieth century design elements persist in the large stock of existing houses reused from generation to generation, the ways of being a family continue to evolve. In more than 90 percent of the homes in the L.A. study, the small kitchens of yesteryear rank among the top three spaces used by family members. Indeed, the kitchen often ranks first.

So despite their spatial limitations, these older kitchens always bustle with activity. In fact, we find that room size is a poor predictor of how and with what frequency L.A. families use the kitchen. Smaller kitchens often host more traffic than larger ones.

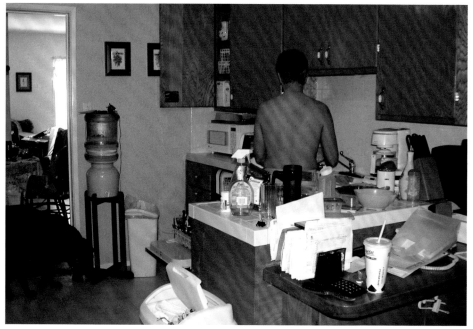

> This is our kitchen where I spend a lot of my time! I like spending time in here 'cause I like to cook a lot. I just wish it was a little bit bigger because I have to have people in the kitchen when I cook.
>
> **Mother (Age 40), Family 12**

RANK OF KITCHEN AMONG FREQUENTLY USED ROOMS

Graph legend:
- ● 1ST
- ■ 2ND
- △ 3RD
- ○ UNRANKED

Y-axis: SCAN SAMPLING OBSERVATIONS OF FAMILY MEMBERS IN KITCHEN (0%, 10%, 20%, 30%, 40%, 50%)

X-axis: SIZE OF KITCHEN (SQUARE FEET) (50, 100, 150, 200, 250, 300, 350)

Remodeled Kitchens

As shown in the graph above, most of the large kitchens in the L.A. study (those >175 square feet) are the most intensively used rooms in their respective houses. Even many smaller kitchens (including those with washers and dryers) share this high rank.

The four largest kitchens (280+ square feet) in the study have been remodeled by current or previous homeowners, and they are the most frequently used spaces during the workweek at those homes. Investments in the expansion and renovation of kitchens seemingly reflect the inadequacies of kitchen space in older American houses and the desire to accommodate a wide range of everyday family activities. Despite their frequent and intensive use, however, we found that kitchens are not the most common house remodeling project. Far more of the L.A. families have chosen to overhaul their old bathrooms and master bedrooms.

Will future archaeologists be able to detect the ways parents and children used their kitchens during the early twenty-first century, even though kitchen walls may define a small space unchanged since the 1940s or 1950s? We think they will, and this chapter highlights how the material record of kitchen experiences is highly patterned and implicates a culture of "busyness" that is now synonymous with middle-class, dual-income U.S. households. These kinds of findings are completely missed by time-diary studies and other large-scale sociological and economic surveys of family activity.

But first we turn to another question: why are kitchens so central to the coordination of everyday family life?

KITCHENS AS HEARTHS

Since the Paleolithic era, humans and their ancestors have gathered around the hearth to process and share food, one of the most symbolically important substances in our material repertoires. Because we take food into our physical selves, the practices surrounding its preparation and eating are deeply personal ways of interacting with the environment. The physiological, ideological, and social importance of food brings us time and again to the hearth, a place where food is most effectively prepared.

The hearth, the campfire, the bread oven—all have been for millennia the places where people exchange information, spin stories, transmit histories, and socialize children regarding how to interact with foods and how to be a member of the culture. Indeed, an orientation to the hearth as a place of provisioning, warmth, safety, learning, and social interaction may be deeply ingrained in the human psyche, accounting in part for why people in modern industrial nations still gravitate to the kitchen.

> This is the kitchen, where I spend a lot of my evenings. Besides my full-time job as a parent, this is my other full-time job—in the kitchen.
>
> **Mother (Age 28), Family 8**

THE KITCHEN TABLE

Kitchen tables and islands are intensively used furnishings. Our scan sampling data show that these localities, no matter how small, host the widest array of daily activities in the house. Children and parents hold conversations and do homework, work-related tasks, bill paying, scheduling, and eating there.

In 11 of the 12 houses that feature a table in the kitchen and a table in the dining room, the kitchen furniture is more frequently used, even when the dining room table surface is larger. Indeed, in nearly 80 percent of the houses in the Los Angeles study, kitchen or kitchen-adjacent spaces that feature tables are either the most or second-most intensively used spaces in the home.

Children in many families do their homework at the kitchen table or island counter, even when functional desks are available in their bedrooms. Opportunities for family members of dual-income households to spend time together on weekdays are largely limited to the three to four hours after parents and children return home from work or school and before the kids go to bed. Our data indicate that many families consequently adopt the strategy of gathering in kitchen spaces so they can maximize time together while children pursue schoolwork and parents attend to meal preparation or other household tasks. Kitchen tables afford opportunities for interaction amid the demands of jobs, school, and the family.

FAMILY 27

BUILT: 1947
SPECS: 2 bed, 1 bath
AREA: 1,206 square feet
RESIDENTS: 4

Arturo (age 43)
Ann (age 41)
Claribel (age 8)
Jonas (age 5)

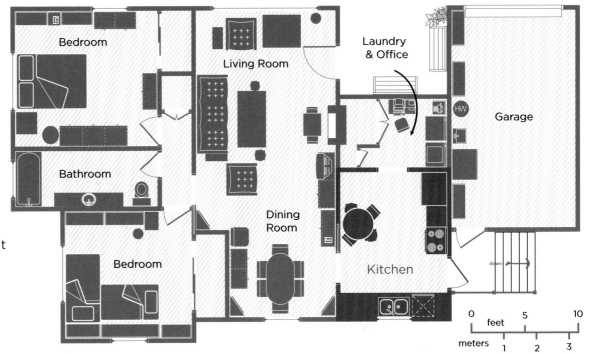

> " Here's the kitchen, which is not a bad size. I mean, it has degraded with time. One thing that we kind of miss here, that we don't have a lot of, is counter space. It is ((pause)) full of a lot of other things. Sometimes when we cook, I would like to have more space, but this is what we have right now.
>
> **Father (Age 43), Family 27**

Families typically favor small kitchen tables, like this one in the Family 27 home, over larger dining room tables, even when the latter are very close to the kitchen. Photographic, video, and observational data sets independently implicate kitchens as central to maintaining family cohesion and to coordinating everyday activities.

Kitchen tables and island counters usually contain high proportions of temporally sensitive artifacts. On weekday mornings, assemblages of objects on those surfaces reflect activities performed on the spot (e.g., reading the newspaper) as well as activities that are anticipated to occur outside the home (e.g., submission of schoolwork). The morning assemblage of ephemera is different from that recorded during afternoon and evening uses of the kitchen. In this sense, we regard kitchen table and counter surfaces as anticipatory spaces, or places where family members stage the food, tools, and possessions to be used at a later time and in other spaces. As parents and children return home during the late afternoon, the arrays of objects that appear help define the evening activities in the kitchen.

Other kitchen surfaces accumulate objects and equipment essential to daily family operations, including PDA devices, mobile phones, work planners, writing equipment, and the like. Nearly every kitchen features a similar assemblage, either on a countertop or a small stand, and typically adjacent to a wall calendar, a telephone, and a vertical surface for posting various bills, notices, and other important paperwork. That these objects are so consistently located in kitchen spaces speaks volumes about the centrality of kitchens in the daily experiences of American dual-income families.

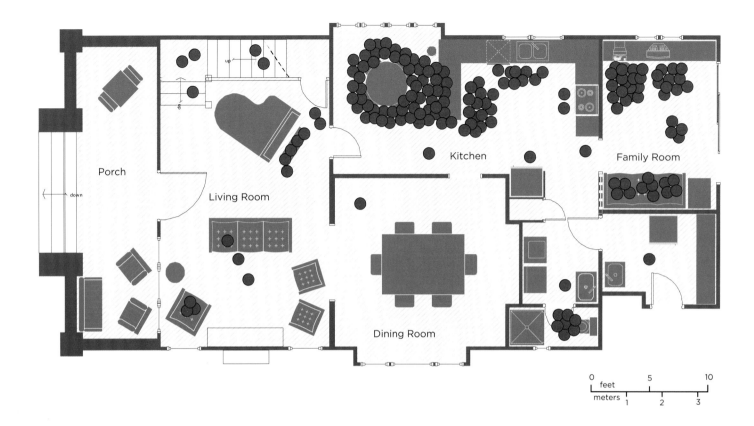

FAMILY 11

BUILT: 1912
SPECS: 3 bed, 1 bath
AREA: 2,035 square feet (2 levels)
RESIDENTS: 4

Frederick (age 41)
Rich (age 41)
Amy (age 9)
Andrew (age 6)

SCAN-SAMPLING OBSERVATIONS OF FAMILY MEMBERS' LOCATION

Each red dot on this map represents the location of a parent or child in the Family 11 household as observed every 10 minutes over the course of two weekday afternoons and evenings. Here, we overlay the aggregate set of our person-centered observations—thereby collapsing a span of eight hours—into a single map (map depicts the downstairs of this two-story house).

The patterns that emerge are striking: fully two-thirds (68 percent) of the family's use of space on weekdays is concentrated in two rooms, with the kitchen (48 percent) emerging as the single-most intensively used space. Activities in the family room (20 percent) typically involve the TV or the computer. Upstairs bedrooms (n=3) account for 18 percent of observations, and the remaining home spaces are used even less (range = 1–6 percent). Very intensive use of kitchen spaces is not just confined to Los Angeles. Time-diary data collected from 500 families in eight American cities reveal that working families throughout the U.S. are spending more time in kitchens than other places at home. This recent study by the University of Chicago Sloan Center lends strong support to our findings.

WEEKDAY SCAN-SAMPLING OBSERVATIONS OF FAMILY ACTIVITIES IN THE KITCHEN

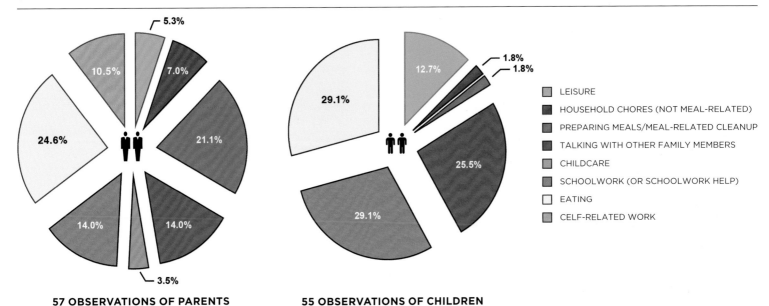

57 OBSERVATIONS OF PARENTS

5.3%
10.5%
7.0%
24.6%
21.1%
14.0%
14.0%
3.5%

55 OBSERVATIONS OF CHILDREN

12.7%
1.8%
1.8%
29.1%
25.5%
29.1%

- LEISURE
- HOUSEHOLD CHORES (NOT MEAL-RELATED)
- PREPARING MEALS/MEAL-RELATED CLEANUP
- TALKING WITH OTHER FAMILY MEMBERS
- CHILDCARE
- SCHOOLWORK (OR SCHOOLWORK HELP)
- EATING
- CELF-RELATED WORK

Parents and children in Family 11 spend time in the kitchen in qualitatively different ways. Eating, of course, is one of the more popular activities for everyone. All of the meals transpire at the kitchen table rather than at the much larger and nearby dining room table. The parents spend much of their time in the kitchen preparing meals and washing dishes, whereas the children spend as much time at the kitchen table doing homework as they do eating. These data make apparent that this family's kitchen—as is true for nearly all families in the study—is an important place for communication and interaction on weekdays.

" We really spend all of our time downstairs... and the kitchen is where we spend the absolute most time, 'cause we do the homework there and everything else. We don't spend a ton of time in the dining room.

Father A (Age 41), Family 11

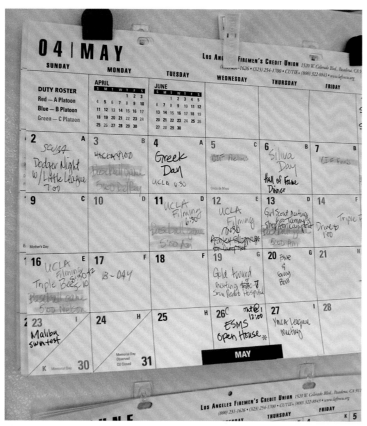

TRACKING TIME

Dual-income families with school-age children must balance numerous competing demands for their time on the typical weekday, including those made by workplaces, schools, sports practice, music lessons, commuting, and household chores. The practice of marking and posting calendars is a nearly ubiquitous solution to the shared problem of accurately recalling, anticipating, and coordinating the complicated schedules of individual family members.

Among the Los Angeles families, we document over 160 posted calendars, with an average of 5.2 calendars per house. Of these, 104 calendars (62 percent) are centrally placed in 29 of the 32 kitchens. The occurrence of multiple calendars in kitchen spaces, many of which are laden with notations, highlights a salient fact of modern family life: parents and children engage in more time-sensitive activities than can be relegated to and reliably recalled by individual memory.

The utility of the simple wall calendar has evolved beyond tracking the days of the month. In a society that places considerable importance on structuring the time allocated to work hours, meetings, and homework, the calendar is among a small assemblage of objects that parents place in kitchens to monitor time and events as they unfold on a daily, if not hourly, basis. This assemblage includes large wall clocks, white boards, cork boards, magnetic boards, and chalkboards.

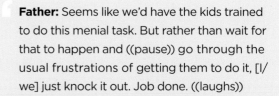

Father: Seems like we'd have the kids trained to do this menial task. But rather than wait for that to happen and ((pause)) go through the usual frustrations of getting them to do it, [I/ we] just knock it out. Job done. ((laughs))

Interviewer: Is it a chore that they are supposed to do?

Father: I don't think it's very well structured. The chore list. The list of duties. So I think they take turns, but it's got to be initiated by my wife saying whose turn it is next. There's too many other things to do.

Interviewer: And it's emptying the dishwasher and putting in the dishwasher? Is that the chore? Or cleaning up after breakfast?

Father: Um—catch as catch can, pretty much. There's no regular sequence of who does it unless we get serious about another schedule. We don't have a schedule right now for these chores.

Father (Age 58), Family 18

The assemblages of objects found in kitchen sinks are also sensitive to the variety of ways kitchens are used over the course of the day. Parents' comments on these spaces reflect a tension between culturally situated notions of the tidy home and the demands of daily life. The photographs reflect sinks at various points of the typical weekday, but for most families, the tasks of washing, drying, and putting away dishes are never done. These are tasks typically shouldered by parents rather than children. In fact, household chores constitute fewer than 3 percent of all children's activities at home. Empty sinks are rare, as are spotless and immaculately organized kitchens. All of this, of course, is a source of anxiety. Images of the tidy home are intricately linked to notions of middle-class success as well as family happiness, and unwashed dishes in and around the sink are not congruent with these images.

06 Bathroom Bottlenecks

OVER THE LAST several decades, many of the most successful American situation comedies have revolved around the humor arising from daily family experiences at home. Popular shows such as *Family Ties*, *The Cosby Show*, *Roseanne*, and *Everybody Loves Raymond*, among others, capture the amusing trials, tribulations, and moments of warmth that characterize the American take on family life. Hollywood depicts ordinary folks in studio-built replicas of kitchens, living rooms, and bedrooms. Underrepresented and often altogether absent from these depictions of "real" family life in "real" homes is perhaps the most contested of home spaces: the bathroom.

Despite the passing of many decades since Archie Bunker famously flushed the upstairs toilet on *All in the Family*, scriptwriters still avoid scenes in bathrooms, perhaps finding the setting too small and too delicate.

This is a missed opportunity to capture not only the humor of bathroom situations but also important cultural processes and family moments happening under the radar there. Generally speaking, Americans do not regard the bathroom as a meaningful or interesting space, although a recent trend in architectural design reimagines the bathroom as a place of luxury and relaxation. People simply classify the bathroom in functional terms. As one L.A. family videotaped a home tour, 8-year-old Josh and his 5-year-old sister playfully summed up the most basic of bathroom activities as a private place for personal bodily functions.

Josh: Okay, this is a bathroom. We really need it—and I got to go right now.
Leslie: Josh! Stop taping!
Josh: Oh, sorry, I forgot. We really need this room because if we didn't we would have to go out in the...
Leslie: Backyard!
Josh: Exactly.

An anthropological lens on bathrooms brings into focus some of the other more subtle ways that these small spaces shape our daily routines as well as our relationships with spouses and children. The bathroom, after all, is the place where a new day begins, where we face the mirror and take stock of ourselves and the day to come. Bathroom inventories include all of the equipment and sundries needed to construct the persona: hair dryers, curlers, styling gels, lipstick, mascara, perfumes, razors, aftershaves, and the like. During these preparations we begin pondering and scheduling the day—meeting with colleagues, picking up groceries, planning an event.

Many American houses feature a single bathroom, and it is often the smallest of all rooms. As such, it is a pivotal place on weekday mornings, an in-demand room where families encounter scheduling bottlenecks. As the images in this chapter show, these rooms are impacted as well by the many objects competing for finite counter space, and several parents complain during their home tours about cramped bathroom spaces. At the same time, small homes can create opportunities for children to learn the importance of sharing and collaboration.

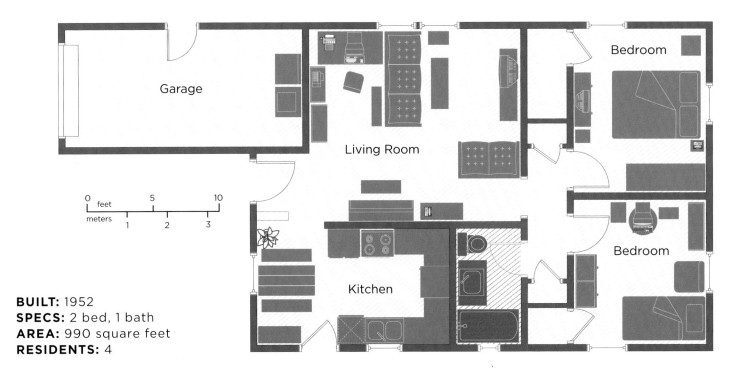

Garage

Living Room

Bedroom

Bedroom

Kitchen

0 feet 5 10
meters 1 2 3

BUILT: 1952
SPECS: 2 bed, 1 bath
AREA: 990 square feet
RESIDENTS: 4

FAMILY 5

Tanner (age 33)
Delphina (age 37)
Aurora (age 8)
Weston (age 5)

BATHROOM AREA = 41 SQ FT

CRAMPED BATHROOMS: THE 32 LOS ANGELES HOMES

Architectural elements of American homes built or remodeled during the last 30 years reflect a shift in the significance of bathroom space, a change that corresponds with the emergence of the predominant new economic model for the middle class: the dual-income household. Most homes in the 32-family Los Angeles sample (87 percent) were built before 1980.

The newer houses (those built since 1980) have an average of three bathrooms, typically measuring nearly 57 square feet each.

Several pre-1980 houses in the study have been remodeled and now feature a mean of two bathrooms. Prior to remodeling, these houses as a group featured just 1.25 bathrooms. The bathrooms dating to the 1970s and earlier have, on average, only 51 square feet of space.

A TYPICAL MORNING IN THE BATHROOM OF FAMILY 5

7:00:43 **7:02:21** **7:06:39** **7:08:14** **7:10:33**

THE MORNING TIME CRUNCH

On weekday mornings, the hallways, kitchens, and bathrooms of dual-earner family homes are every bit as busy as an airport terminal. Like corporate travelers who frantically attend to last-minute messages and calls before boarding planes, parents and children must complete numerous preparatory tasks before flying off to work and school. Showering, brushing teeth, packing lunches, assembling homework, scheduling—these are among the common activities to be completed during the moments between the morning wake-up call and the inflexible departure hour.

Our scan sampling data indicate that some families dash through their weekday morning routines in as few as 30 minutes. However, the average time needed to organize and mobilize everyone is 74 minutes, and some households' morning routines require more than two hours. During this period, the territory in the bathroom becomes a scarce and contested resource. Families must coordinate and negotiate with diplomacy to avoid clashes. At Los Angeles homes with a single bathroom, demand is highest between 7:00 and 7:45 a.m.

> Only one bathroom. When we add on [to the house] we want to add a new bathroom. Four of us with, you know, one sink and one toilet and a shower... sometimes there can be a real backup of people waiting to use the facilities in here.
>
> **Father (Age 33), Family 5**

SITES OF SOCIALIZATION

One bathroom, two working parents, three school-age children... and only limited time to get everyone through the bathroom routine, out the door, into the car, and off to school and work. The fast-paced flow of morning preparations often encounters a bottleneck—a major scheduling crunch—at the bathroom.

While the constraints of space and time imposed by single-bathroom homes are fixed, most of the families in our study demonstrate flexibility and inclusiveness in their morning routines. Although not without occasional hiccups and longings for personal privacy, parents' strategies for mobilizing children on weekday mornings effectively coordinate overlapping needs for the bathroom space. It is not uncommon to see dad shaving while a 10-year-old with a toothbrush in his mouth hunches over the sink and a younger sibling gets ready to use the toilet. Parents often use these overlapping bathroom moments to teach children self-care practices.

In short, simultaneous bathroom use not only solves the morning time crunch but also serves as an opportunity for parents to socialize their children, demonstrating basic values centering on civility and hygiene. Children learn how to take turns, how to be considerate of others' needs, how to respect privacy, and how to share limited resources. To this extent, single-bathroom homes can play a pivotal role in helping parents instill the idea that the needs of the family come before those of the individual.

> " And there's the shower that I share with my brother. We both have to share this bathroom, which is kind of annoying.
>
> **Daughter (Age 17), Family 4**

ACROSS AMERICA

When surveyed in 2008, American adults reported spending an average of 30 minutes in the bathroom each day. One-quarter of the U.S. population claims to use the bathroom for more than one hour per day.

A robust 88 percent of Americans divulge that they use electronic devices, including cell phones and computers, while in the bathroom.

Almost half of Americans surveyed (47 percent) claim to clean their bathroom(s) at least once per week.

> This is where the sports section gets read every morning. See that litter box? The cats do their thing down there. So I get to share the bathroom with the cats.
>
> **Father (Age 58), Family 18**

07 Master Suites as Sanctuaries

MASTER BEDROOMS in U.S. homes were rather unremarkable during the first two-thirds of the twentieth century. Most were not much larger than other bedrooms in the home, and few were conjoined with a bathroom. Only within the last few decades have middle-class Americans redefined their relationship with the master bedroom and made it into something more than a space intended for rest and sleep.

Houses built during the later 1900s, especially those constructed since 1980 in the suburbs, reveal a transformation in attitudes about parents' sleeping space. In many of these newer homes, the master bedroom emerged as a considerably larger space adjoining a nice, upgraded bathroom and a spacious walk-in closet. This private, luxurious space— the master suite—symbolizes a modern American ideal of leisure and retreat from the annoyances and fast pace of daily life. This ideal seems largely rooted in *hotel envy*, a yearning for an *en suite* space at home just like chic, upscale hotel rooms we have seen or visited.

Most homes of the middle class in the greater Los Angeles region do not have such spaces despite the fundamental changes that have occurred in the workforce and the prominent place of master suites on homeowners' wish-lists. These families live in the large stock of homes built before the 1970s–80s. A good number of the households in the L.A. study pursued remodeling as their best option to remove unwanted, old architectural configurations.

Home remodeling in the United States morphed into a whole new kind of industry during the 1990s. Dozens of television shows, magazines, and websites catered to homeowners' desires to transform their homes and appealed to a popular new do-it-yourself ethos. Whether licensed contractors or owners did the work, millions of advertising dollars promoted services and products (e.g., sinks, cabinets, storage systems, decks) to the average homeowner. During the early- to mid-2000s, U.S. consumers spent an average of $100.4 billion each year on major home additions, alterations, and improvements to the property. Some $58.7 billion (58 percent) of this figure was poured into homes built prior to 1980.

At the 32 Los Angeles houses, among the many spaces targeted for remodeling, master bedrooms proved the most popular, constituting about one-fourth of all remodeling projects by current or previous homeowners. In most cases this was a substantial investment. Overhauling master bedrooms is costly: in the mid-2000s, the average expanded master bedroom or new master suite of modest scale in Los Angeles cost just over $80,000. This hefty price tag approaches or exceeds parents' combined annual salaries for many of the families in the study. Furthermore, just 60 percent of this expense is typically recouped when the house is sold. By contrast, home sellers could expect to regain greater than 90 percent of costs entailed in minor kitchen remodeling.

Another cost linked to investing in master bedrooms/suites is that they are not spaces integral to the everyday juggling of household chores, meals, schoolwork, or work done from home. In fact, our time in families' homes made it startlingly apparent that these spaces often sit empty. On weekday afternoons and evenings, master bedrooms are rarely occupied prior to children being put to bed. In the few instances when family members occupy these spaces, use of the room is transitory. The scan sampling data document, for instance, a parent or child occasionally walking through the space to put away clothes or retrieve an object. Our video data reflect the same. At a handful of homes, a computer in the master bedroom attracted a bit more activity.

In contrast, most of the L.A. kitchens are bustling and rather cramped centers of family activity that could benefit from modest upgrading or remodeling. Yet only 10 percent of all remodeling projects targeted kitchen spaces. So why are parents prioritizing master bedrooms over other home spaces, particularly kitchens? Our data suggest that parents with young children seek to create a space that is insulated from the daily activities that occur in the rest of the home.

Among the families in our study, the hours between arriving home on weekday afternoons and children's bedtime may be experienced as a taxing extension of the workday. Job- and school-related projects still need to be completed, childcare and household chores demand attention, and time must be invested in coordinating schedules and other logistical planning. The kitchen features multiple visible reminders of planning and chores, and it and the rest of the house may be peppered with clutter, a clear source of stress.

Master suites, on the other hand, may symbolize an escape from it all. Often at the end of long hallways distancing them from other rooms, master suites are envisioned as private spaces with the potential to confer restorative benefits to weary parents—a place of respite from obligations and expectations. Our photographic records and measurements show that in the L.A. sample, remodeled master bedrooms are of course larger than their unremodeled counterparts, and they often feature a comparatively low density of furniture and other possessions, creating a less cluttered look. Many of these spaces contain a television and bear strong similarities to the suites found in upscale hotels. Indeed they were likely patterned after that expensive, "spa-like" style, and the implicit links with vacation, getting away, and pampering/luxury all reinforce the feeling that the reinvented master space is the parents' home sanctuary. If only they had the time to use it!

> " Okay this is our bedroom [and] we love it. We used to really have a small one. And now we got a big one, so we're real happy with that.
>
> **Father (Age 43), Family 25**

MASTER SUITES AS SANCTUARIES   111

FAMILY 12

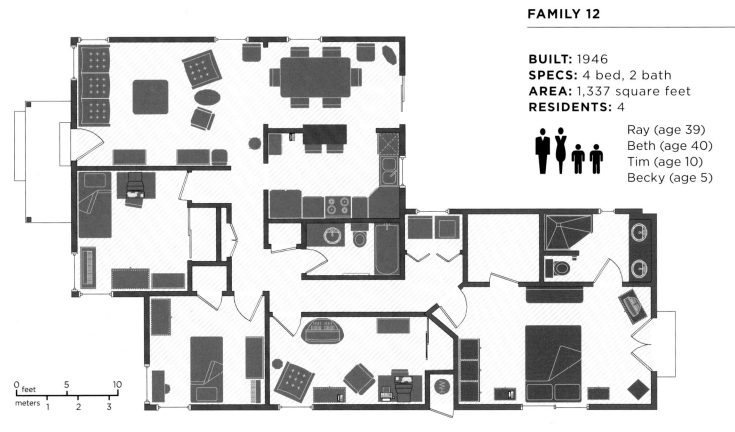

BUILT: 1946
SPECS: 4 bed, 2 bath
AREA: 1,337 square feet
RESIDENTS: 4

Ray (age 39)
Beth (age 40)
Tim (age 10)
Becky (age 5)

0 feet 5 10
meters 1 2 3

MASTER SUITE AREA = 312 SQ FT

MATERIAL TRACES OF REMODELING: 32 LOS ANGELES HOUSES

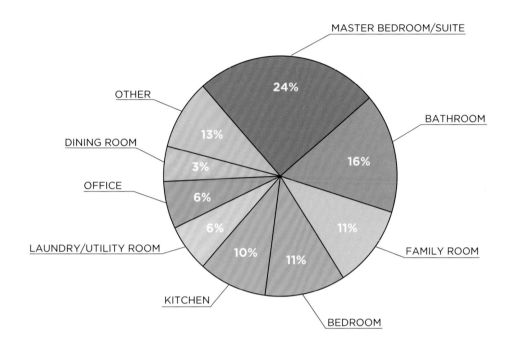

MASTER BEDROOM/SUITE 24%

OTHER 13%

DINING ROOM 3%

OFFICE 6%

LAUNDRY/UTILITY ROOM 6%

KITCHEN 10%

BEDROOM 11%

FAMILY ROOM 11%

BATHROOM 16%

Los Angeles families take on remodeling projects with great zeal, and master suites clearly lead the way. Only 7 of the 32 houses are untouched by the remodeling trend. In the remaining 25 houses, we found evidence for 69 remodeling projects, all entailing major alterations to existing architecture, such as the full addition of a master suite (opposite), complete with spacious walk-in closet. Not all of the identified projects were executed by current home occupants, but most were, and a handful were in progress during the study. Nearly all owners of the houses built before 1980, particularly the smaller homes, muse about remodeling projects they hope to do when time and budgets allow.

> This [bathroom] is another one of my pride and joys. Here we have our Jacuzzi tub... and here's our big shower. We designed all of this bathroom, and we really like it here in the morning. This is where I spend from five thirty to about six, getting ready for work every morning.

Mother (Age 42), Family 4

Adding a second and more lavish bathroom to the home may be one of the driving motivations to remodel the master bedroom into a master suite. Competition for bathroom time can be fierce, and a master bathroom considerably alleviates family scheduling pressures on weekday mornings. A newfound sense of hotel-caliber luxury is also part of the package. Many of the Los Angeles families have created bathroom additions that feature two sinks and an assortment of objects that help to impart a spa-like feel, including scented candles, decorative soaps, and potted plants.

Owners of older homes frequently voice a desire for additional bedroom space. Master bedrooms in unremodeled houses are often too small to comfortably accommodate king beds, multiple dressers, and other furniture. Introducing cribs for infants and toddlers into the space may test the absolute limits of such bedrooms, heightening parents' perceptions of crowding and confinement.

In the Los Angeles study, however, families that create master suites with more ample space do not always gain the restorative benefits that they bargained for. Several families living in homes with expanded master bedrooms simply spread more clothing and possessions over a wider area. And as is evident in the newly designed master suite at left, young children sometimes sleep in these spaces, so not all parents can enjoy their private "refuges" during the years when they may most need them.

08 Plugged In

AT NO POINT during tens of thousands of years of human history have people been as deeply engaged with nonessential technologies as we are today. Ownership of devices associated with entertainment and mobile communication has escalated from fad to addiction. The numbers and diversity of consumer electronics that U.S. households purchase, use, and discard are unprecedented, a pattern that extends as well to most other postindustrial societies around the globe. So it is not surprising that policy makers and analysts link current rates of innovation, production, and consumption of electronic and digital technology to growing concerns regarding climate change, dwindling reserves of nonrenewable resources, community health, and an array of other social issues.

The design and marketing of consumer electronics increasingly promote lifestyles centering on televisions, cell phones, and laptop computers as well as the numerous services that support them. The evolution of these devices has been astoundingly rapid.

When Maxwell Smart first opened his shoe phone to talk with his boss on *Get Smart* in 1965, who knew how prescient a moment it was. By the mid-1980s, mobile phone technology in the U.S. was a reality but still a novelty, limited to bulky radiophones hardwired into high-end automobiles and popularized through hip, syndicated television shows such as *Miami Vice*. Few households had access to this kind of technology, and most Americans had yet to hear the term "cellular" as a modifier of "telephone."

Two decades later, nearly 85 percent of adults use cell phones, up from 53 percent in 2000. More revealing is the fact that 59 percent of U.S. adults age 18–29 years now consider the mobile phone an absolute requisite for everyday life.

As consumers came to view multiple electronic and digital devices as necessities rather than luxuries, the significance of digital media among American households exploded. Age and income clearly have influenced how intensively adults used these objects through the years, but the fact that most Americans are now routinely plugging in to available streams of mass media is incontrovertible.

Social science research examining the impact of digital technology and media in American lives has expanded almost as rapidly as consumer interest in these products. But we do not yet fully understand the ways that elevated uses of digital media are shaping cognitive and social development among children, or how such activities affect our relations to loved ones or the world beyond.

Our ethnographic experiences in Los Angeles households, including observations of the numbers, types, and locations of consumer electronics in the home and the ways they are used, introduce wholly new kinds of data to the discussion. The systematic examination of family interaction with media technologies reveals not only how often digital media are used at home but also in some depth how digital lifestyles are intrinsic to what it means to be an American family.

TELEVISION AND DAILY LIFE

Around the world, ownership of television sets has grown rapidly since the 1980s. Peter Menzel's photographic survey of household possessions documents at least one TV in the possession of 21 of the 30 families he has chosen to represent as "typical" households in 30 countries. Only five of the 30 families depicted own two or more TVs, including a family from Pearland, Texas. In a handful of cases, the TV is prominently displayed next to or between parents and children—appearing on sofas, important chairs, and even in a canoe during the carefully staged photo sessions. One might justifiably interpret the television as an inanimate but cherished family member.

In North America, and in as few as three generations, mass media broadcast by analog and digital signal has all but replaced oral history and become the primary conveyor of culturally shared ideas. Broadcast communication, particularly television-streamed content, figures so prominently in economic decisions, political outcomes, and moral reasoning that even at the height of the last U.S. recession, TV advertising expenditures exceeded $50 billion. Television is now so intricately woven into the fabric of the American family experience that few children born during the last two decades will be able to imagine a social world that has not been partly shaped by the imagery, discourse, and ideas originating from television programming. In fact, many twenty-first century children are born in the physical presence of a TV: most labor, delivery, and recovery rooms in the U.S. now feature large, wall-mounted flat-panel sets. That TVs are witness to such intimate and emotionally bonding experiences speaks volumes about televisions and the American way of being.

Currently, 99 percent of U.S. households own a TV, and more than 50 percent own three or more. All of the families in our study have at least one TV, and most have two or more. One set is typically located in a large space used by all family members, such as the living room, family room, or den. The set used by the collective is a compelling example of an object that is not merely a tangible product of otherwise invisible cultural forces but rather an agentive participant in the daily production of social lives. The introduction of a new TV to a living room, for example, shapes the decisions underlying where we locate our furniture, where we direct our gaze, and how we orient our bodies.

At some deeper cognitive level, our relationship to the TV—which includes a relationship to the object itself but also our personal experiences centering on TV media—even shapes the ways that we relate to our built spaces. Our photographs of living room assemblages repeatedly reveal spaces organized around televisions rather than spaces with other primary affordances, such as face-to-face conversation. For all of its influence on the design and organization of space, the TV may as well be a hearth, which until quite recently in human history exerted the most influence on the spatial distribution of social interactions and activities inside homes. Indeed, families often locate the TV immediately adjacent to a wood-burning stove or fireplace, and new homes feature recessed fireplace-like nooks designed for television sets. The TV has ascended to the rank of essential major appliance (alongside the refrigerator, clothes washer, and dryer) around which builders and architects imagine the designs of residential spaces.

Families now also routinely equip various bedrooms with televisions. Fully 25 of the 32 CELF families (78 percent) have a TV in the parents' bedroom, and 14 families (47 percent) place a TV in one or more of the bedrooms used by children. Researchers at the Kaiser Family Foundation surveyed 1,051 U.S. households with young children and found that 43 percent place a TV in at least one child's bedroom.

The same Kaiser-funded project reveals that 87 percent of children age four to six years are able to turn on the TV without assistance. Most two- and three-year-olds can do the same (82 percent), and the majority of children belonging to both age groups are capable of changing the channel. Suffice it to say that American children learn how to operate and engage with the TV at a very young age, a fact that has motivated more than 4,000 studies addressing the impacts of TV on children, education, and the social lives of families.

These impacts, however, are debated. Some researchers associate TV viewing with reduced social interaction, while others report the opposite and even see evidence for families' use of TV time as a platform for togetherness. Research based on our unique observational data sets is new to the discussion and actually lends support to both generalizations, reflecting the complex relationship Americans have with television. For example, our study shows that families are not actively engaging with TV as much as we might otherwise predict. Attentive, focused TV viewing accounts for only 11 percent of all primary person-centered scan sampling observations, and the careful coding of 380 hours of videotape (derived from our observational videography) reveals that families engage with TV media on weekday afternoons and evenings for an average daily total of just 46 minutes (although the TV may be turned on for much longer periods). Furthermore, families' viewing is usually a social experience: during about two-thirds of observations where a child or adult watches TV, at least one other family member is present.

However, children are slightly more likely than their parents to watch TV alone. Kids view solo in about 17 percent of the cases where we record TV viewing as the primary activity; mothers and fathers watch alone in only 6 percent and 13 percent of the cases, respectively. We also found that children much more frequently watch TV in a bedroom (34 percent of primary TV observations, alone or with others) than either of their parents (9 percent for mothers and 10 percent for fathers). Indeed, the socially isolating potential of TV appears higher among families that have more than one TV set in the home. Children in families that have TVs in one or more bedroom spaces are more likely to watch TV alone than children in families that do not have a TV in a child's or parents' bedroom.

> I think Cartoon Network is essentially poison. Left to his own devices [my son] will watch TV for four hours at a time.
>
> **Father (Age 40), Family 29**

THIRTY-TWO LOS ANGELES HOUSEHOLDS: NINETY-NINE TELEVISIONS

The percentage of households with three or more televisions in our study is the same as that observed for U.S. homes as a whole (56 percent). As this figure shows, only two of the L.A. households feature just one television, and larger families tend to have more TVs. Our data show that most of the five-person households contain three or more TVs, and two of these families have six or seven.

Not surprisingly, families place most of their TVs in living rooms and family rooms. Yet fully 25 of the 32 parents' bedrooms also feature a television, and 22 children's bedrooms (representing 14 households) contain a television set.

Parent's Bedroom: 25

Living Room: 23 Outbuilding: 1

Playroom: 2 **Child's Bedroom: 22**

Family Room: 11 Garage: 4

Home Office: 6 Guest Bedroom: 2

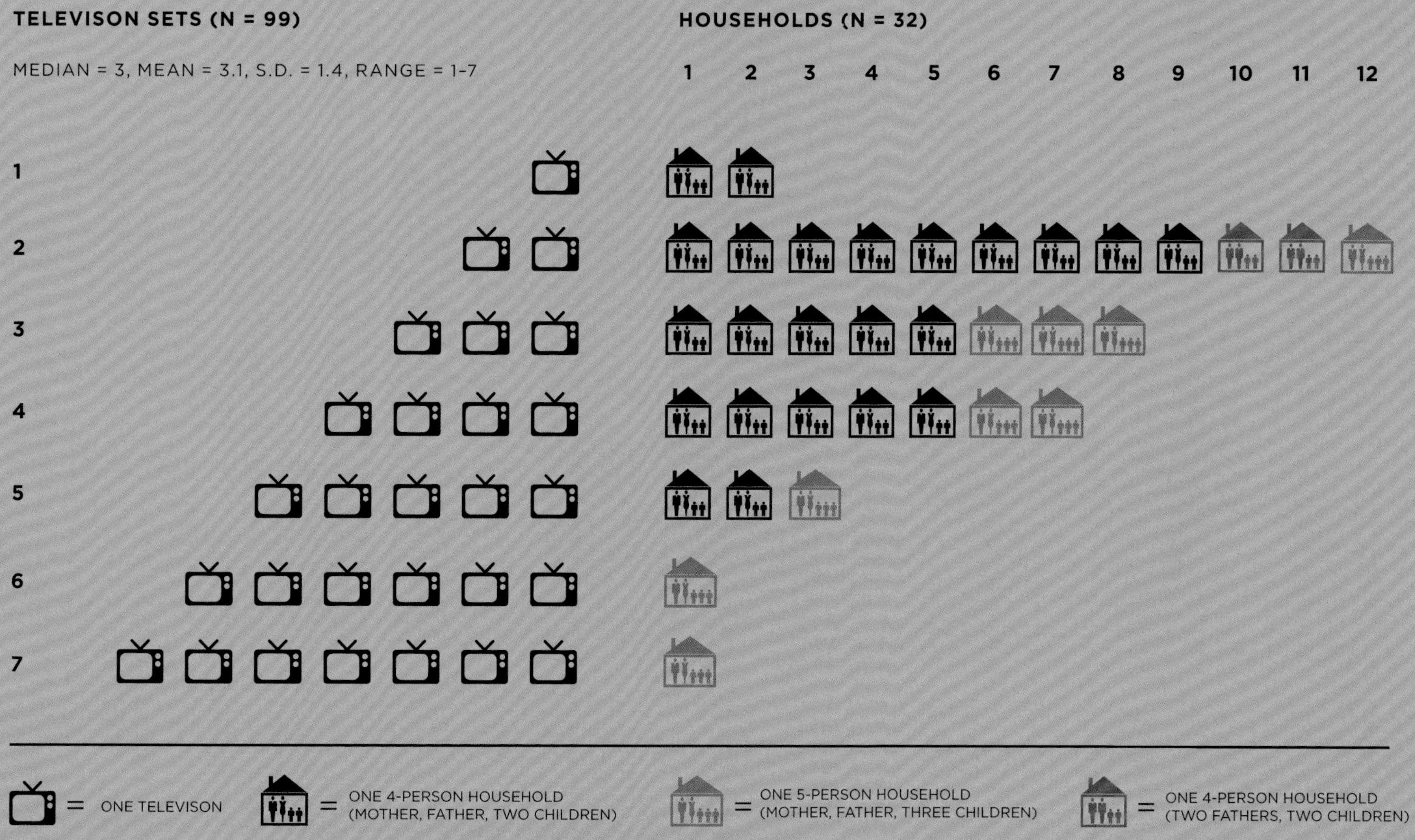

TELEVISON SETS (N = 99)

MEDIAN = 3, MEAN = 3.1, S.D. = 1.4, RANGE = 1–7

HOUSEHOLDS (N = 32)

| 1 | 2 | 3 | 4 | 5 | 6 | 7 | 8 | 9 | 10 | 11 | 12 |

Legend:
- = ONE TELEVISON
- = ONE 4-PERSON HOUSEHOLD (MOTHER, FATHER, TWO CHILDREN)
- = ONE 5-PERSON HOUSEHOLD (MOTHER, FATHER, THREE CHILDREN)
- = ONE 4-PERSON HOUSEHOLD (TWO FATHERS, TWO CHILDREN)

THE MATERIAL LEGACY OF TV

The proliferation of video media technology since the debut of network television in 1946 has had a profound influence on American lifestyles. Indeed, few Americans can imagine everyday life without access to TV. Television is so entrenched in popular culture that we are surprised when we meet people who do not have at least one set. In 1947, U.S. households owned 44,000 TVs, just one set per 3,275 people. During the early 2000s, people purchased about 31 million TVs annually in the U.S., or one new TV for every nine Americans each year.

Of course, sales figures do not reflect the number of sets already found in what archaeologists regard as systemic context (here, the home): the behavioral system in which artifacts participate in everyday life. The full inventory of TVs emerges only when the count includes the sets purchased in years past and still in the house. Only some older TVs are replaced. As is true for most artifacts, the life history of each individual television is entangled in the changing ways that families use them, the availability of similar artifacts in the home, and the desire for newer forms of visual media technologies.

Eventually the life history of a TV, or at least the portion of the life history that overlaps with family use, comes to an end. At that point, the artifact exits the systemic context and enters an archaeological context, a state in which interaction is primarily with the natural environment, such as the city dump. The Environmental Protection Agency estimates that during the mid-2000s, Americans discarded an average of 1.5 billion pounds of TVs each year, in the range of 25 to 27 million sets annually, of which only 4 to 4.5 million were collected for domestic recycling.

The EPA also reports that about 200 million computer products and 100 million cell phones and PDAs joined TVs in dumps each year in the mid-2000s. Municipal solid waste landfills will be goldmines of future archaeological inquiry.

Most families in the Los Angeles study were using cathode ray tube (CRT) television sets, with a few rear-projection units scattered among households. Flat-panel TVs gained popularity after 2004, and the conversion to digital stream media undoubtedly resulted in an even faster rate of TV discard during the last half of the decade.

TAKING INVENTORY OF U.S. TV SETS (AS OF 2009)

TVs sold since 1980	772 million
TVs in use	312 million
TVs in residential storage	104 million
Old-model TVs ready for disposal	356 million

AN ARCHAEOLOGY OF TVs

The rate at which TV technology evolves and the sheer volume of television sets people discard both suggest that this artifact will be particularly useful for teasing out discrete generations of household refuse from the materially complex and jumbled strata that constitute our municipal landfills. Archaeologists rely on seriation—the sequencing of functionally similar artifacts based on stylistic differences—as a method for ascertaining relative chronology at archaeological sites. Although seriation cannot be used to pinpoint a specific date, it places older and younger materials in order based on the simple assumption that object styles change over time. Frequency seriation thus determines the relative age of each layer.

We expect 1980s-era landfill strata to contain high proportions of black-and-white TVs and color CRT TV sets, but very low proportions of rear-projection TVs and no flat panels. Garbage layers forming today will contain few black-and-white sets, numerous color CRT sets, and (assuming a continued low rate of recycling) an increasing number of flat panels, assuming that household disposal of any particular TV may postdate its purchase by a decade or more.

Archaeologists often use battleship curves to depict frequency seriation patterns. These graphs are particularly useful for showing changes in the proportion of different technological styles of artifacts over time. Interpretation of the curves is straightforward: the width of a horizontal bar for each year represents a percentage of a total count (see right axis opposite). In 1990, for example, 22.6 million TVs were purchased in the U.S. Only 6 percent were black-and-white sets, whereas 46 percent were color CRT models less than 19 inches in size and another 46 percent were large color CRT models. Just 2 percent were the new rear-projection models, and flat panels had not yet debuted.

The shape of each battleship curve is particularly telling, providing an at-a-glance account of changes in the popularity of an artifact style or type over the course of its history. After the artifact's introduction, curves typically become gradually wider as the artifact style becomes more popular. As newer styles enter the material system, the first curve tapers and eventually terminates altogether. The maximum widths and rates of tapering (in both directions) summarize the popularity, rapidity of change in preference or supply, and persistence through time.

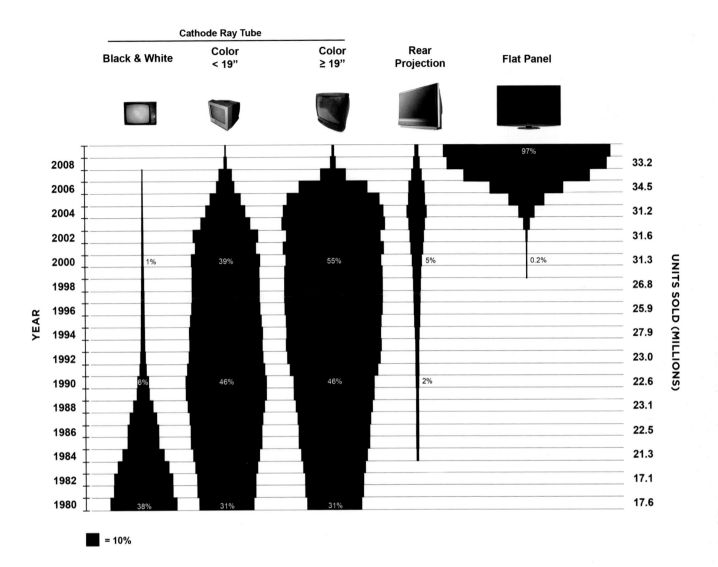

Cathode Ray Tube

| Black & White | Color < 19" | Color ≥ 19" | Rear Projection | Flat Panel |

YEAR						UNITS SOLD (MILLIONS)
2008					97%	33.2
2006						34.5
2004						31.2
2002						31.6
2000	1%	39%	55%	5%	0.2%	31.3
1998						26.8
1996						25.9
1994						27.9
1992						23.0
1990	6%	46%	46%	2%		22.6
1988						23.1
1986						22.5
1984						21.3
1982						17.1
1980	38%	31%	31%			17.6

■ = 10%

In the complex story of U.S. television consumption, several well-defined patterns emerge. Black-and-white TV sets persisted until the early 2000s, long after color CRT sets began dominating household assemblages, and rear-projection units enjoyed a long lifespan but never gained popularity. When significantly better TV technology emerged in the form of flat-panel models, color CRT models declined precipitously, producing the narrow profiles at the tops of the CRT battleships. The adoption rate of flat-panel sets has been steep and unprecedented in the domain of television technology, expanding as CRT use plummeted.

Between 2006 and 2009, U.S. landfills received 1.2 billion consumer electronic devices at an average disposal rate of 293 million units per year.

GENERATIONS OF GAMERS

Television broadcast and cable programming are the predominant forms of media purchased and used by dual-income families with children. Computer and video games are second. In 2002, the production and sale of computer and video games in the U.S. was a $6.4 billion industry, and by 2011 that industry generated more than $25 billion in revenue. Nearly three-fourths of American households are now gaming in digital space.

According to a recent survey by the Entertainment Software Association, the average computer and/or video game player is 37 years old. In fact, nearly 30 percent of all gamers are at least 51 years old. Although this may be surprising, those born in the late 1960s and early 1970s—many now parents—were the first to grow up with video game consoles, including Atari, Commodore 64, NES, and Sega. This first generation of teenage arcade and console gamers came of age around the time when the original PlayStation was debuting on the shelves of U.S. retail stores. Parents in 45 percent of U.S. households play computer games or console-based video games with their children at least once per week.

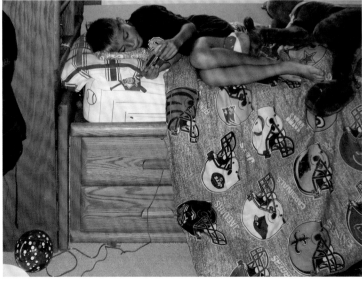

Americans have thrown out roughly 3 billion pounds of computing equipment during the last few decades.

Video games can be played on many platforms, including gaming consoles hooked to TVs, portable game systems, smart phones, and computers, with and without Internet access. Our time with the Los Angeles families preceded the advent of the smart phone, but computers and game consoles were nearly ubiquitous in these homes, and many children used portable game players. Hundreds of our photographs reflect the accretion of a wide range of objects around computers and game consoles, including peripheral devices (printers, hard drives, speakers), floppy disks, software CDs, controllers, surge protectors, and hundreds of linear feet of tangled power cords and data cables.

The sheer mass of computing-related equipment in families' homes is paralleled outside the house by a computing infrastructure that by 2003 included more than 39 million miles of fiber-optic cable line in the U.S. Recent estimates suggest that the search-engine giant Google employs about 1 million servers to accommodate online Internet use.

In many homes, long histories of gaming are evident in accumulated collections of older-generation consoles and controllers near TVs. Despite U.S. data that suggest otherwise, among the Los Angeles families we observe mostly boys and sometimes fathers playing video games. Scan sampling reveals that girls engage more frequently with computer games as opposed to console games, but our photo archive rarely captured mothers or daughters playing either console- or computer-based games.

Gaming is often a social and collaborative activity, although it is occasionally at the center of play-related conflicts concerning whose turn it is or which game to play. Video gaming—or we might argue TV watching in general—frequently prompts parent-child conflicts concerning the completion of homework. Various schoolwork items strewn on the floor await the attention of the boys pictured above.

Mother: I've got some strict rules about TV and video [games] around the house... and now it's more strict.

Interviewer: What are they?

Mother: I took away all of the boy's game controls for the whole week. I did let Jake have them back today since it was a half day... but [with the understanding that] there would be limited time now and on the weekend. We used to let them play and we used to just take their word that they didn't have any homework or anything to study for... But now I call other kids' parents to get the scoop on what there is... like a spelling test every Friday or a vocab test every Friday or, you know, that kind of thing. Because we really have to do something.

Interviewer: So during the week no video games?

Mother: No. Nothing. No TV unless I see that their work is all done. And they've studied for everything. They do get to choose one program for half an hour before bedtime... whether it be as soon as they get home or right before bed. One half-hour program.

Mother (Age 50), Family 18

Careful scrutiny of the ethnographic video archive documenting the weekdays of the Los Angeles families reveals that, on average, children spend more time on gaming consoles (22 minutes per weekday) than on computers (15 minutes). Neither of these figures is as large as anticipated by previous studies. Children are gaming about 7 percent of their weekday time at home.

Nonetheless, the time spent gaming (solitary or collaborative) cuts quite substantially into the roughly 4 hours of overlapping time parents and children have in the home on weekday afternoons and evenings.

We rarely observed parents engaging with computers or gaming consoles. During the period of our study with each family, parents' average time at the computer was 7–8 minutes, and their average time spent gaming on consoles was 1–2 minutes. They use computers mostly for work-related tasks but also communicating with friends and family (e.g., e-mail). Overall, parents are so busy attending to childcare, meal preparations, and other household chores that there is precious little time to spend plugged in when children are at home and awake. This is particularly true for parents with infants and toddlers. Fathers enjoy only marginally more computer and console time (2 minutes, on average) than mothers.

My Space, Your Space, Our Space: The Personalization of Home

THE IMPULSE TO SURROUND OURSELVES with things we value may be a human universal. Referring to the possessions at his home in Chile and the deep connection he felt to them, the Nobel Prize–winning poet Pablo Neruda wrote this verse:

They told me
many things, everything.
Not only did they touch me
and take the hand I gave them
but they were bound to my life
in such a way
that they lived in me
and were such a living part of me
that they shared half of my life
and will die half of my death.

Homes around the globe contain lifelong accumulations of possessions. People acquire heirlooms, art, souvenirs, and photos that hold deep, personal meaning and play an important role in defining who they are. As this chapter illustrates, these and certain other classes of objects are especially central to individual and family identities in industrial-era, consumer societies.

Across the U.S., every home on every block is its own small, informal museum with a unique set of material culture filtered from a wider spectrum of available art, furnishings, and technologies. Americans display many of their most cherished possessions in the "public" rooms

of houses because they assist in telling family histories and expressing what is most important about family members. Picture the unambiguous message about homeowner identity transmitted to a visitor entering the house of a language teacher who has French provincial furniture and a painting of the Eiffel Tower over her fireplace. The car enthusiasts next door display Indy 500 memorabilia and large paintings of vintage Porsches in the living room. And so on down the street.

Of course, each local cultural tradition plays a role in shaping the numbers and kinds of things people acquire and how they arrange them to create a fulfilling home environment. In some societies, households accrue few objects, and the places where they are used and stored tend to be fairly standardized across households. But when household possessions proliferate, there is a much greater material basis for the flourishing of individual variation, echoing a wide range of different family identities.

Houses of the American middle class are larger and contain substantially more material goods than those of other societies. The per capita acquisition of objects in the U.S. has expanded every decade since the early twentieth century. Shoppers have access to a dizzying variety of inexpensive goods, providing ample raw material for personalizing the home. Objects situated throughout the house bespeak family aesthetic choices, interests, and affiliations. The objects placed in the main rooms where parents greet and entertain guests, from the foyer to the living/family/dining rooms, have the highest signaling potential. These are the optimal places to communicate information about family identity to both insiders and outsiders.

The American legacy is the house as personal statement, materialized by as many dazzling and identity-projecting possessions as can be afforded.

THE ZEAL TO PERSONALIZE

As long ago as 1890, the American home had become a place for artistic expression and the projection of family ideals in ways quite different from customs in other western nations. Emerging then were enduring societal expectations that women should make the house attractive, decorating with art and furniture that imaginatively conveyed family tastes and personal identities. The house was the main stage for self-expression and creativity.

New and sumptuous department stores such as Macy's and Marshall Field's offered seductive assemblages of goods that women could purchase to display. These objects signaled refinement, taste, and status, associating the family with famous designers. Americans set out on a course of intensive shopping fueled by the ornate Victorian style of that era. Homes of the well-to-do and middle class alike featured paintings, mirrors, elaborate wallpaper, heavy drapes, tufted furniture, and shelves crowded with crafted items.

The need to select decorative objects that conform to ideals of home beauty at the same time that they project family individuality—that is, the family's personality—fostered a competitive approach to home decorating that has gone unconstrained for 120 years. Social critics of the early 1900s skewered the middle class and characterized these early manifestations of "showing off" behavior as domestic exhibitionism and conspicuous consumption.

Today, U.S. families still seek distinctive looks for their homes but also emulate designs seen in popular media and at houses of admired or wealthy neighbors. Emulation of widely advertised styles leads, of course, to duplication of home furnishings and goods, so tensions always arise between imitation and creativity in decorative choices.

> Let's see, and there are our walls! Our colorful walls. The magenta wall, the blue wall, the green wall. So we have this color thing going in our house. It makes it more alive, more fun to to live in. And I think it's good for our kids to grow up with a lot of color. We'll see when they grow up what happens, but I know I would have loved it if I had a house like that.
>
> **Mother (Age 48), Family 1**

IDENTITY AND POSSESSIONS

Early twenty-first century home personalization extends well beyond art and decorative items. The numerous things middle-class Angelinos display serve to visibly align the family with various nations, religions, professional sports teams, schools, and entertainers. Objects on display also highlight victories and accomplishments in sporting and educational activities, trace family histories by means of photographs, and draw attention to the family's accrued "cultural capital." In this last category we might find souvenirs from a trip to Australia or a collection of antique glassware that demonstrates worldliness or a degree of mastery of a subject.

Many home-based material displays are fundamentally tied to family heritage, and the things people decorate with when starting their own households often reflect (or reject) what they have been socialized to admire at parents' and grandparents' houses. An heirloom, for instance, may stimulate an interest in Art Deco or Scandinavian design that blossoms into the family "style." Residents then strategically place objects of high communicative value in visually accessible places to convey that history and style to all who enter the home. A simple statistical analysis of the Los Angeles data reveals no significant correlation between income or education and counts of aesthetic objects in public rooms of houses, which suggests that the impulse to display in these places is widely shared across economic levels.

In California, exterior house design (mid-century, Spanish, ranch, boxy 1980s) very often fails to convey much about family identity. In a society where families buy new houses every few years, architectural types may be completely disconnected from interior style choices and aesthetic values. We really must get inside to explore family identity.

The typical L.A. home is a crowded canvas of personal and familial expression—with a few spare and minimalist households in the mix. This chapter is a guided tour through the history-rich spatial environments of twenty-first century homes.

> This shadeless lamp belonged to my grandma, my Grandma Sydney, who I really loved a lot, and I have a lot of her things in the house and they really mean a lot to me.
>
> **Mother (Age 48), Family 1**

> This was a clock that was Aunt Herta's that Jerry inherited when Aunt Herta passed away. It's very old and quite valuable, and he really, really, really likes it. I think it's kind of cool, too.
>
> **Mother (Age 41), Family 16**

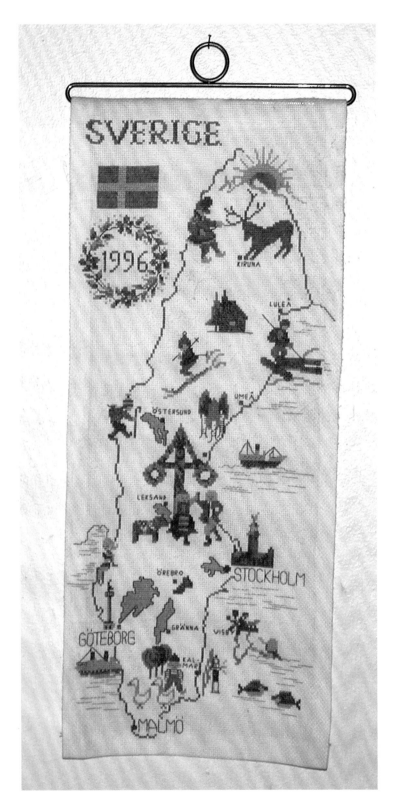

EXPRESSIONS OF AFFILIATION

Quite a few parents in the Los Angeles study identify with a specific cultural heritage or religion, and they prominently display material markers in the home that signal their affiliations. A Swedish-American mother hangs a Swedish flag over the front door and a large painting of a seascape from Sweden in the living room. A deeply religious family has "I Love Jesus" on the bathroom soap dish and biblical passages posted around the house. A Brit features a flag from England on an office wall, and Japanese-American parents display delicate figurines from Japan in a living room cabinet. Even the refrigerator doors in some households feature flags and religious symbols.

> That's the patron saint of Cuba... and we have a clock here with the Last Supper.
>
> **Father (Age 33), Family 5**

Americans identify fervently with their religions and their sports teams alike. Here we see typical materializations of these interests.

Many of the L.A. families align with people or teams in the music, film, and sports worlds, the symbols of popular culture with whom they feel strong affinities. Posters of rock and sports stars and sports team pennants and banners are prevalent artifacts.

The Los Angeles Lakers basketball team and Dodgers baseball team are represented by displays of flags, posters, and helmets in just under 20 percent of households. These kinds of objects convey the message that family members participate actively in shared communities of fans.

> Here's my handsome son, and this is his room here. He's very lucky to have this great room because he's got all of this sports memorabilia here. A lot of it, well most of it, is signed and numbered, and he got this from his uncle who passed away.
>
> **Mother (Age 42), Family 4**

More than 13,000 U.S. companies make and engrave trophies. It is a multi-billion dollar industry.

TROPHIES

Trophies, ribbons, plaques, beauty contest tiaras, and certificates are ubiquitous in bedrooms and home offices. Children's accomplishments are the most frequently featured. In 31 of 32 homes in the study, diplomas, trophies, and other insignia of personal accomplishments of the children are on display, announcing competitive success. One in six families in the L.A. study also feature trophies in living rooms and family rooms.

ART AND COLLECTIONS

Relatively little original wall art is displayed in the houses in the Los Angeles study: we document about three formal artworks per house in the living/family/dining rooms. But the major pieces succinctly express who the families are and what they value.

ACROSS AMERICA, young families early in the household life cycle typically display affordable decorative objects such as souvenirs and prints. Major investments in art or collections are often postponed until the family matures, sheds expenses, or accrues savings.

> "
> There's a beautiful painting a friend of ours did, which I love. The interior of the coffee cup is the wall. I think that's really neat.
>
> **Mother (Age 48), Family 1**

> "
> And this is my one of my pictures I bought. I love this picture. I got it at a garage sale for 40 bucks and it was appraised around $2,500 to 3,000 dollars!
>
> **Mother (Age 42), Family 4**

> This is a piece by a friend of ours who died from AIDS many years ago. And he did a series of pieces, he made cards out of them, postcards with sayings on the back that became therapy for people with AIDS and other life-threatening illnesses like cancer. They'd look at the picture... and discuss how they were feeling.

Father A (Age 46), Family 10

> When we moved in this wall was painted all types of psychedelic colors and images, as if people had a big painting party inside the house. We have started covering it up and eventually we're going to have either wallpaper or paneling. Some people come in and say they like it, but we didn't paint it, so we don't like it. We just ignore it.

Father (Age 33), Family 5

> We have a very strong cat motif in this house. We have three cats.

Father (Age 33), Family 5

> Celia loves to collect all of these Disney items and she has all these pictures of her... with her friends and stuff like that.
>
> **Mother (Age 42), Family 4**

> That vase we brought back with us from Peru when we adopted the kids, so that has a particular significance. Some of the other pieces are just art. And this photo is one of several photos we have by a good friend of ours. And so it has significance because we know the artist very well; known him for years.
>
> **Father A (Age 46), Family 10**

Three-dimensional pieces such as human and animal figurines, pottery, glassware, and vases are the most common decorative objects in these households. Within the foyers and living/family/dining rooms, we find an average of about 20 per family, with as few as none and as many as 85. Beyond their aesthetic appeal, these objects convey information about places and cultures the family has "collected" in its travels.

" [Here's] an antique piece passed down through my family that I adore, and I love waking up and walking into my home and seeing it every day. It reminds me of my childhood.

Mother (Age 38), Family 3

Heirloom furnishings and art objects occupy prominent places in dining rooms and living rooms. Side-by-side with these treasured objects, U.S. families often choose to display mass-produced, non-original figurines and other items (some in the kitsch category) such as Disney characters, dolls, and vacation mementos like a miniature Taj Majal or Northwest Coast totem pole. The common impetus to do this likely emerges from a need to participate in a broad community of consumers of popular culture that Americans find comfortable. Such items also enjoy wide appeal because the investment in dollars is minimal as families materially document the museums and places they have been. Such markers of travels and interests allow us to forgo acquiring the cultural capital—the specific art-history training—that would be needed to purchase authentic, high-end art pieces or ethnographic arts from distant lands.

> Here is our dining area. That chandelier was passed down to me. I spent many a dinner—Shabbat dinners, high holidays—with my siblings looking through the mirrored glass making faces. And now I see my children doing that, so it's a special piece to have.
>
> **Mother (Age 38), Family 3**

CHILDREN'S ART

Just over half of the Los Angeles families display children's art alongside purchased, formal art in the house's most public rooms: the living/family rooms, dining rooms, and foyers.

Of these families, five stand out: Family 28 has 12 pieces of their children's art in the dining room and family room, and four other families display 5 to 10 pieces each. They collectively account for 38 of the 59 children's art pieces observed across all public rooms in the study.

The more customary spots for kids' art are children's bedroom walls and in groupings with snapshots and other ephemera on refrigerators, cabinets, and bulletin boards in kitchens.

Pre-teens and teens in the U.S. build self-identity as they devote attention to musicians, athletes, TV characters, and animals in popular child-oriented films. The process of identity construction is materialized by means of images of these icons on bedroom walls.

Among the L.A. families, posters and clippings of pop culture figures are nearly universal, found in 29 of 32 houses. Posters and kids' art are arranged very informally in bedrooms, revealing children's own agency in selection and display.

NAME DISPLAYS

Children also express themselves and assert claims to personal space at home by posting prominent name emblems on bedroom walls, bulletin boards, doors, and desks. One child's room has no fewer than six name emblems. Name displays, trophies, photos, and posters all assist in establishing children's emerging personal identities.

FAMILY PHOTOS—FAMILY HISTORIES

Los Angeles families display an average of 85 photos throughout the house.

If the house is an instrument of display for family history and memory, the single most emphatic way this is materialized in the U.S. is through family photographs. The prevalent custom in Los Angeles households is to display dozens of photos, and the images families select for display celebrate a wide spectrum of ordinary moments as well as the extraordinary events in each family's life. These images put a clear stamp of "this is ours" throughout the home.

Each house in the L.A. study features at least 10 family photographs. We are much more likely to find 80 to 90, however, and some families display more than 200. Places such as the fireplace mantel, living room walls, and hallways are standard locations for the most important framed photos, often formal in subject matter (such as weddings, studio portraits, school pictures) and adjacent to art.

When baby boomers were growing up, most middle-class households did things differently. Modest numbers of selected formal school, wedding, and military portraits were placed in living rooms, but the flood of less momentous pictures of pets, parties, dinners, vacations, and other day-to-day events did not gain such front-stage display. Other departures from past display practices are evident. Families today not only choose far greater numbers of photos to exhibit, and the great majority are informal, but also these photos are given prominent display space in a wider array of rooms than was formerly the case. Families with school-age children typically place photos in at least four or five rooms on walls, desktops, shelves, and bulletin boards.

Clusters of small framed snapshots are particularly ubiquitous on tables and shelves in living/family rooms, home offices, foyers, and bedrooms—even garages and bathrooms. Another informal locus for snapshots is the kitchen, especially the refrigerator and kitchen cabinets.

So amid the jumble of images, middle-class families share practices related to the spatial placement of their photos. Consciously or not, they often link several attributes when they choose a spot for a particular photo. These features are: formality and visibility of the house space (public front-stage rooms versus informal back-stage rooms such as bedrooms); formality of the display surface (wall or mantel versus bedroom desk); formality of the photo subject (school portrait versus picnic); and formality of the frame. A typical formal wedding picture is large and nicely framed, it is in the living room, and it is on a wall or treasured piece of furniture. A typical snapshot from a vacation is a small, casually framed print on a bedroom shelf or an end table in the family room.

Although photo displays are commonplace in the U.S. home, they are not typical elsewhere in the world. Indeed, our collaborators who have analyzed photos in Swedish, Italian, and Peruvian households document their rarity. Formal photos of ancestors and transformative events such as weddings are present, but displays are small and do not spread throughout the house. In Naples, Italy, photos of any living family members are rare, and photos of ancestors are displayed primarily in outdoor religious shrines.

> " And all the walls are covered with family pictures. It's the wall of honor.
>
> **Father A (Age 46), Family 10**

> In here we have some of our pictures. This picture up here on the wall is a friend of mine, and he's a professional photographer. So we really like those pictures... Right there is a picture of my dad the day that Dale and I got married, so we really like that... And then, let's see... the kids. That's the picture of them over on Catalina, our favorite place to go.

Mother (Age 42), Family 4

These pictures are all very meaningful to us—to me—to us. This was a surprise party that Jerry threw for me when I was pregnant with Allison in New York City. That's my brother next to me and my mom, who flew up from Florida to be there with me—with us. I didn't know that they had flown up to New York. It was a pretty big deal. That was for my thirty—what would that be? Thirty-first birthday? Jerry and I on Christmas in Pensacola, Florida, on the beach. That's a picture Jerry and I took of ourselves, holding the camera up while we were dating. We really like that one.

Mother (Age 41), Family 16

> Here is the wall of photos. It's all of our relatives and it's all of our relatives' children... I do enjoy looking at that, and I often reference it when talking about our relatives to the kids.

Father (Age 41), Family 1

> Our wall of photos, of all of our relatives, our great-grandparents, our grandparents, our mothers, our fathers. These are my great-grandparents from Russia. This is my grandma and grandpa. This is my mom; it's a neat picture... That's my dad. I love that photo. It's really super cool.

Mother (Age 48), Family 1

THE ARCHAEOLOGY OF US

Because material culture impacts human lives every minute of the day, wherever we are, systematic documentation of spaces and things is central to unpacking the fundamental workings of this (or any) society. Yet only rarely does an opportunity arise to explore, in great depth, the layers of daily life and rich microscale of activities within the houses of a complex culture.

Houses are the foundation of the American dream, and we have seen how the assemblages of objects that families purposefully accumulate and arrange in them preserve and legitimize personal histories. Middle-class America has the most possessions per family in history, and, to no one's surprise, people enjoy a house brimming with valued things. Decades of competitive consumption, aggressive marketing tactics, and low inflation-adjusted prices for goods have fueled these cultural norms. Aspirational spending—including fortunes spent on children's material wants and desires—reached new heights prior to the 2008 recession.

We have no obvious way to actually measure the importance of material goods to family well-being, purpose, and sense of achievement, but if something happens that results in the disappearance of these things, there is no doubt that the loss is overwhelming. When a disaster like Hurricane Katrina strikes, the destruction of the house and possessions, in families' own words, has the effect of extinguishing family history. Time and again, homeowners say: "It's all gone now. I lost my home. I lost my identity."

A lesson emerging from the L.A. study is that while material affluence signals personal pleasure and economic success, it also entails hidden costs, including the comfort lost if possessions overly crowd a home. The full impacts of consumerism—good and bad—on L.A. families have not yet been sorted out. But this study clearly points toward several major trends—waning outdoor leisure time, unprecedented and often burdensome clutter, reduced social interaction at mealtimes, clashing schedules, the invasion of kids' material culture into all corners of the house, stockpiling, and more—that require close examination in the broader U.S.

Americans zealously guard their privacy, and few people ever see the personalized and historicized interiors of their neighbors' homes. From the streets, we see only the visual cues that homeowners choose—such as landscaping and cars—to convey their attitudes toward the community. Scientific access to the private recesses of people's homes has always been fleeting, small in scale, and particularistic. The details of daily activities and material goods of the U.S. middle class remain mostly unseen.

We change that story, unveiling the home lives of 32 Los Angeles families. Important differences exist among these ethnically, occupationally, and financially diverse California households, yet it is not a contradiction to say that they share behavioral and material characteristics that help to define what it is to be a two-income, middle-class family in the twenty-first century. No archaeologist would fail to recognize the striking material signature of AD 2001–2005 America a thousand years from now.

LIST OF PHOTOGRAPHS

ENDNOTES

Chapter 1

Page 3. Quote regarding modern material culture studies: William Rathje 1981:54.

Page 3. Sociological examination of household objects: Mihaly Csikszentmihalyi and Eugene Rochberg-Halton 1981.

Page 4. Studies of American work and spending trends: Juliet Schor 1991, 2004.

Page 4. Historical studies of consumerism, housing, identity: Russell Belk 2001, Judith Flanders 2003, Dolores Hayden 1984, Clare Cooper Marcus 1995, Witold Rybczynski 1986, Thorstein Veblen 1899.

Page 4. Intensive consumerism in U.S.: Robert Frank 2010, Annie Leonard 2010, Peter Stearns 2006, Elizabeth Warren 2006, Peter Whybrow 2005.

Page 5. Women's shopping: Meghan Daum 2010.

Page 5. Sociological studies during the 1960s: David Halle 1993, Marcus Felson 1976.

Page 5. Household assemblages of 30 nations: Peter Menzel 1994.

Page 5. Photographers noted for images of homes and possessions: Frederic Brenner and Yehuda Amechai 1998, Jeff Dunas 2001, Walker Evans 1938, Bill Owens 1973.

Page 8. Early ethnoarchaeological studies: Lewis Binford 1978, Robert Janes 1983, Susan Kent 1984.

Page 9. Early modern material culture studies: Richard Gould and Michael Schiffer (editors) 1981, William Rathje 1979, William Rathje and Cullen Murphy 1992, Michael Schiffer 1999.

Page 16. Detailed discussion of CELF methods: Elinor Ochs, Anthony Graesch, Angela Mittman, Thomas Bradbury, and Rena Repetti 2006.

Chapter 2

Page 24. U.S. toy consumption: International Council of Toy Industries 2010.

Page 26. Clutter and stressful settings, Los Angeles study: Darby Saxbe and Rena Repetti 2010.

Page 31. Book sales: Peter Lyman and Hal Varian 2003; U.S. Bureau of the Census 2002.

Page 31. Toy sales: U.S. Department of Commerce 2006.

Page 31. Music CD sales: International Federation of the Phonographic Industry 2004.

Page 31. DVD Figures and VHS sales: Motion Picture Association of America 2007.

Page 31. Apparel and footwear sales: American Apparel and Footwear Association 2004.

Page 32. Barbie facts and statistics: Barbie Collectors Guild 2008.

Page 36. Distribution of the world's children: Thomas McDevitt and Patricia Rowe 2002.

Page 36. U.S. toy consumption: International Council of Toy Industries 2010.

Page 36. Grandparent expenditures on children: AARP 2002.

Page 37. Categories of toy sales: U.S. Department of Commerce 2006.

Page 44. Uses of garage space, Los Angeles study: Jeanne Arnold and Ursula Lang 2007, Anthony Graesch 2006.

Page 44. Storage industry data; by 2010, these figures had ballooned to 2.22 billion square feet and 1 in 10 homeowners: Self Storage Association 2011.

Page 50. Psychologists evaluating clutter: David Tolin, Randy Frost, and Gail Steketee 2007.

Chapter 3

Page 53. Rate at which U.S. corporations introduce processed food products: Eric Schlosser 2001: 124.

Page 54. McDonaldization process: George Ritzer 2004.

Page 54. Fast-food history and patronage by U.S. adults: Eric Schlosser 2001.

Page 54. Dinner food sources, Los Angeles study: Margaret Beck 2007.

Page 55. Dinner preparation time, Los Angeles study: Margaret Beck 2007.

Page 56. Fathers' work hours and commute times: Anthony Graesch n.d.

Page 56. Dinner preparation data, Los Angeles study: Margaret Beck 2007.

Page 57. Frozen food aisles in grocery stores: Emily York 2011.

Page 58. Teen obesity rates: Leslie Samuelrich 2010.

Page 59. Home-cooked foods and health: health interviews, Los Angeles study 2001–2005.

Page 60. Eating dinner together, U.S. survey data: Betty Klinck 2010.

Page 60. Dinnertime togetherness, Los Angeles study: Elinor Ochs, Merav Shohet, Belinda Campos, and Margaret Beck 2010.

Page 61. Fragmented, short dinners, Los Angeles study: Elinor Ochs, Merav Shohet, Belinda Campos, and Margaret Beck 2010.

Page 61. American and Italian perceptions of food: Elinor Ochs, Clotilde Pontecorvo, and Alessandra Fasulo 1996.

Chapter 4

Page 69. Time-diary data on TV watching 1960s–90s: John Robinson and Geoffrey Godbey 1997.

Pages 69–70. Indoor leisure time, Los Angeles study: Margaret Beck and Jeanne Arnold 2009.

Page 70. Analyses and surveys of leisure time, U.S. data: Suzanne Bianchi, John Robinson, and Melissa Milkie 2006; Peter Whybrow 2005.

Page 70. Statistical analysis of time use: Nora Broege, Ann Owens, Anthony Graesch, Jeanne Arnold, and Barbara Schneider 2007.

Pages 70–74. Diminished outdoor leisure, Los Angeles study: Jeanne Arnold and Ursula Lang 2007.

Page 71. Evolution of home and yard space in U.S.: Dolores Hayden 1984.

Page 78. Back yard data, Los Angeles study: Jeanne Arnold and Ursula Lang 2007.

Chapter 5

Page 81. Age profile of Los Angeles houses: U.S. Bureau of the Census 1997.

Page 81. Kitchens as backstage and gendered spaces: Erving Goffman 1959, Rudi Laermans and Carine Meulders 1999.

Page 84. Symbolic importance of food: Anthony Graesch, Julienne Bernard, and Anna Noah 2010.

Page 86. Intensity of kitchen use, Los Angeles study: Anthony Graesch 2009.

Page 86. Opportunity for interaction between parents and children, Los Angeles study: Belinda Campos, Anthony Graesch, Rena Repetti, Thomas Bradbury, and Elinor Ochs 2009; Anthony Graesch n.d.

Page 91. Temporally sensitive kitchen objects: Anthony Graesch 2009.

Page 92. Time-diary data on kitchen use, 500-family study: Nora Broege, Ann Owens, Anthony Graesch, Jeanne Arnold, and Barbara Schneider 2007.

Page 94. Time-tracking objects: Anthony Graesch 2009.

Page 96. Parents' and children's contributions to household chores, Los Angeles study: Wendy Klein, Anthony Graesch, and Carolina Izquierdo 2009; Darby Saxbe, Rena Repetti, and Anthony Graesch 2011.

Chapter 6

Page 100. Los Angeles housing data: U.S. Bureau of the Census 1997.

Page 101. Weekday morning bathroom routines: Anthony Graesch n.d.

Page 103. Child socialization in small homes: Marie Hartwell-Walker 2008.

Page 104. Survey of American activities in bathrooms: American Standard 2008.

Chapter 7

Page 107. Los Angeles housing data: U.S. Bureau of the Census 1997.

Page 107. Remodeling expenses by job type and year: U.S. Bureau of the Census 2008a, b.

Page 107. Costs of remodeling master suites: Sal Alfano 2004.

Page 109. Master suites as symbolically charged spaces: Anthony Graesch 2006.

Page 113. Remodeling project categories: Anthony Graesch 2006.

Chapter 8

Page 117. Popularity and use of cell phones and digital media in American households: Aaron Smith 2010, Paul Taylor and Wendy Wang 2010.

Page 119. Television ownership around the world: Peter Menzel 1994, Belia Thomas 2003.

Page 119. Television advertising revenue in the U.S.: Carl Howe 2009.

Page 120. Television ownership in the U.S.: Nielsen Media Research 2009.

Page 120. Locations of TVs, Los Angeles study: Darby Saxbe, Anthony Graesch, and Marie Alvik 2011.

Page 120. Toddler and child interaction with the TV: Victoria Rideout and Elizabeth Hamel 2006.

BIBLIOGRAPHY

Page 122. Impacts of television on parent-child social interaction: David Bickham and Michael Rich 2006; Gene Brody, Zolinda Stoneman, and Alice Sanders 1980; Nicholas Dempsey 2005; Elisa Pigeron 2009; Kelly Schmitt, Kimberly Woolf, and Daniel Anderson 2003; Elizabeth Vandewater, David Bickham, and J. H. Lee 2006.

Page 122: Videotaped time spent watching TV, Los Angeles study: Elisa Pigeron 2009.

Page 122. Social context of TV viewing, Los Angeles study: Darby Saxbe, Anthony Graesch, and Marie Alvik 2011.

Page 123. Households with three or more TVs: Nielsen Wire 2012.

Page 124. Television broadcasting in the U.S.: Robert Shagawat 2011.

Page 124. U.S. population in the 1940s to early twenty-first century: U.S. Bureau of the Census 1999, 2010.

Page 124. Systemic and archaeological context: Michael Schiffer 1987.

Page 124. Electronics sales, storage, and discard: Environmental Protection Agency 2011.

Page 125. TV sales, storage, and discard: Environmental Protection Agency 2011.

Page 126. TV sales by type: Environmental Protection Agency 2011.

Page 127. Vintage TV graphic: http://ro-tock.deviantart.com/gallery/?offset=24#/d19ash8 :dev ro-stock:.

Page 127. Discard of electronics devices: Environmental Protection Agency 2011.

Page 128. Sales of video game consoles and their use by parents and children: Entertainment Software Association 2011, Nielsen Wire 2009.

Page 130. Disposal of computing equipment: Environmental Protection Agency 2011.

Page 131. Miles of fiber-optic cable: Robert Hassan 2004.

Page 131. Google servers: Jonathan Koomey 2011.

Page 133. Videotaped time spent gaming and on computers, Los Angeles study: Elisa Pigeron 2009.

Chapter 9

Page 135. Pablo Neruda verse: Luis Poirot 1990:54.

Page 136. American houses, nineteenth and twentieth centuries: Clifford Clark 1986, Peter Thornton 1984, Thorstein Veblen 1899.

Page 137. Counts of art objects in middle-class homes: Angela Orlando 2010.

Page 142. Data on the U.S. trophies and awards industry: Awards and Recognition Association 2010.

Page 156. Documentation of family photographs, Los Angles study: Jeanne Arnold n.d.

Page 157. Family photographs in other nations: Angela Orlando 2010, Heather Loyd, personal communication 2011.

AARP
2002 The Grandparent Study 2002 Report. Electronic document, http://assets.aarp.org/rgcenter/general/gp_2002.pdf, accessed June, 2009.

Alfano, Sal
2004 2004 Remodeling Cost vs. Value Report. Electronic document, http://www.remodeling.hw.net/remodeling/2004-cost-vs-value-report.aspx, accessed December, 2005. *Remodeling Magazine.*

American Apparel and Footwear Association
2004 An Annual Compilation of Statistical Information on the U.S. Apparel and Footwear Industries: Annual 2004. Electronic document, http://www.apparelandfootwear.org/UserFiles/File/Statistics/Trends2004Annual.pdf, accessed September, 2009.

American Standard
2008 American Standard Bathroom Habits Survey Shows We're Multitasking, Even in the Bath. Electronic document, http://www.americanstandard-us.com/pressroom/, accessed October, 2009.

Arnold, Jeanne E.
n.d. Mountains of Things: The Impacts of Consumerism and Clutter. In *Fast-Forward Family: Home, Work, and Relationships in Middle-Class America,* edited by Elinor Ochs and Tamar Kremer-Sadlik, University of California Press, Berkeley. In press.

Arnold, Jeanne E., and Ursula A. Lang
2007 Changing American Home Life: Trends in Domestic Leisure and Storage among Middle-Class Families. *Journal of Family and Economic Issues* 28:23–48.

Awards and Recognition Association
2010 Awards and Recognition Association. Electronic document, http://www.ara.org/about/history.cfm, accessed September, 2010.

Barbie Collectors Guild
2008 Barbie Fun Facts. Electronic document, http://barbiecollectors.thelittleusedstore.com/facts.html, accessed September, 2009.

Beck, Margaret E.
2007 Dinner Preparation in the Modern United States. *British Food Journal* 109(7):531–547.

Beck, Margaret E., and Jeanne E. Arnold
2009 Gendered Time Use at Home: An Ethnographic Examination of Leisure Time in Middle-Class Families. *Leisure Studies* 28(2):121–142.

Belk, Russell W.
2001 *Collecting in a Consumer Society*. Routledge, New York.

Bianchi, Suzanne M., John P. Robinson, and Melissa A. Milkie
2006 *Changing Rhythms of American Family Life*. Russell Sage Foundation, New York.

Bickham, David S., and Michael Rich
2006 Is Television Viewing Associated with Social Isolation? Ropes of Exposure Time, Viewing Context, and Violent Content. *Archives of Pediatric and Adolescent Medicine* 160: 387–389.

Binford, Lewis R.
1978 *Nunamiut Ethnoarchaeology*. Academic Press, New York.

Brenner, Frederic, and Yehuda Amechai
1998 *Exile at Home*. Abrams, New York.

Brody, Gene H., Zolinda Stoneman, and Alice K. Sanders
1980 Effects of Television Viewing on Family Interactions: An Observational Study. *Family Relations* 29(2):216–220.

Broege, Nora, Ann Owens, Anthony P. Graesch, Jeanne E. Arnold, and Barbara Schneider.
2007 Calibrating Measures of Family Activities Between Large- and Small-Scale Data Sets. *Sociological Methodology* 37(1):119–149.

Campos, Belinda, Anthony P. Graesch, Rena Repetti, Thomas Bradbury, and Elinor Ochs
2009 Opportunity for Interaction? A Naturalistic Observation Study of Dual-Earner Families After Work and School. *Journal of Family Psychology* 23(6):798–807.

Clark, Clifford E.,
1986 *The American Family Home, 1800–1960*. University of North Carolina Press, Chapel Hill.

Csikszentmihalyi, Mihaly, and Eugene Rochberg-Halton
1981 *The Meaning of Things: Domestic Symbols and the Self*. Cambridge University Press, Cambridge.

Daum, Meghan
2010 Hunter, Gatherer, Shopper. *Los Angeles Times* 15 April.

Dempsey, Nicholas P.
2005 Television Use and Communication within Families with Adolescents. In *Being Together, Working Apart: Dual-Career Families and the Work–Life Balance*, edited by Barbara Schneider and Linda J. Waite, pp. 277–296. Cambridge University Press, New York.

Dunas, Jeff
2001 *American Pictures: A Reflection on Mid-Twentieth Century America*. Könemann, Cologne.

Entertainment Software Association
2011 2011 Essential Facts About the Computer and Video Game Industry: Sales, Demographic and Usage Data. Electronic document, http://www.theesa.com/facts/pdfs/ESA_EF_2011.pdf, accessed September, 2011.

Environmental Protection Agency
2011 Electronics Waste Management in the United States Through 2009. EPA 530-R-11-002. U.S. Environmental Protection Agency (EPA), Office of Resource Conservation and Recovery.

Evans, Walker
1938 Exhibit "American Photographs" at the Museum of Modern Art, New York.

Felson, Marcus
1976 The Differentiation of Material Life Styles: 1925–1966. *Social Indicators Research* 3:397–421.

Flanders, Judith
2003 *Inside the Victorian Home: A Portrait of Domestic Life in Victorian England*. W.W. Norton, New York.

Frank, Robert H.
2010 *Luxury Fever: Weighing the Cost of Excess*. Princeton University Press, Princeton, New Jersey.

Goffman, Erving
1959 *The Presentation of Self in Everyday Life*. Doubleday, New York.

Gould, Richard A., and Michael B. Schiffer (editors)
1981 *Modern Material Culture: The Archaeology of Us*. Academic Press, New York.

Graesch, Anthony P.

2006 An Ethnoarchaeological Study of Contemporary U.S. Houses and Households. Working Paper #59. Center on Everyday Lives of Families at UCLA, Los Angeles.

2009 Material Indicators of Family Busyness. *Social Indicators Research* 93(1):85–94.

n.d. At Home. In *Fast-Forward Family: Home, Work, and Relationships in Middle-Class America*, edited by Elinor Ochs and Tamar Kremer-Sadlik. University of California Press, Berkeley. In press.

Graesch, Anthony P., Julienne Bernard, and Anna C. Noah

2010 A Cross-Cultural Study of Colonialism and Indigenous Foodways in Western North America. In *Across a Great Divide: Continuity and Change in Native North American Societies, 1400–1900*, edited by Laura L. Scheiber and Mark D. Mitchell, pp. 212–238. University of Arizona Press, Tucson.

Halle, David

1993 *Inside Culture: Art and Class in the American Home*. University of Chicago Press, Chicago.

Hartwell-Walker, Marie

2008 The Family Bathroom Waltz. Electronic document, http://psychcentral.com/lib/2008/the-family-bathroom-waltz/, accessed October, 2009. Psych Central.

Hassan, Robert

2004 *Media, Politics, and the Network Society*. Open University Press, Berkshire, England.

Hayden, Dolores

1984 *Redesigning the American Dream: The Future of Housing, Work, and Family Life*. W.W. Norton, New York.

Howe, Carl

2009 Advertising Forecast Update: Less TV, More Internet. Electronic document, http://shop.yankeegroup.com/product/342/2009-Advertising-Forecast-Update%3A-Less-TV,-More-Internet, accessed August, 2011. Yankee Group.

International Council of Toy Industries

2010 Global Retail Statistics: World Toy Facts and Figures 2003. Electronic document, http://www.toy-icti.org/resources/industrystatistics.html, accessed June, 2009.

International Federation of the Phonographic Industry (IFPI)

2004 The Recording Industry World Sales 2003. Electronic document, http://www.ifpi.org/content/library/worldsales2003.pdf, accessed September, 2009.

Janes, Robert R.

1983 *Archaeological Ethnography among the Mackenzie Basin Dene*. The Arctic Institute of North America, University of Calgary.

Kent, Susan

1984 *Analyzing Activity Areas: An Ethnoarchaeological Study of the Use of Space*. University of New Mexico Press, Albuquerque.

Klein, Wendy, Anthony P. Graesch, and Carolina Izquierdo

2009 Children and Chores: A Mixed Methods Study of Children's Household Work in Los Angeles Dual-Earner Families. *Anthropology of Work Review* 30(3):98–109.

Klinck, Betty

2010 Survey: 89% Will Eat Family Dinner on Thanksgiving. *USA Today* 23 November.

Koomey, Jonathan G.

2011 Growth in Data Center Electricity Use 2005 to 2010. A report by Analytics Press, completed at the request of the *New York Times*, August 1, 2011. Electronic document, http://www.mediafire.com/file/zzqna34282frr2f/koomeydatacenterelectuse2011finalversion.pdf, accessed September, 2011.

Laermans, Rudi, and Carine Meulders

1999 The Domestication of Laundering. In *At Home: An Anthropology of Domestic Space*, edited by Irene Cieraad, pp.118–129. Syracuse University Press, Syracuse, New York.

Leonard, Annie (with Ariane Conrad)

2010 *The Story of Stuff: How Our Obsession with Stuff is Trashing the Planet, Our Communities, and Our Health—A Vision for Change*. Free Press, New York.

Lyman, Peter, and Hal R. Varian

2003 How Much Information. Electronic document, http://www.sims.berkeley.edu/how-much-info-2003, accessed September, 2009.

Marcus, Clare Cooper

1995 *The House as a Mirror of Self: Exploring the Deeper Meaning of Home*. Conari Press, Berkeley, California.

McDevitt, Thomas M., and Patricia M. Rowe
2002 The United States in International Context: 2000. Census 2000 Brief, C2KBR/01-11. Electronic document, http://www.census.gov/prod/2002pubs/c2kbr01-11.pdf, accessed September, 2009. U.S. Census Bureau.

Menzel, Peter
1994 *Material World: A Global Family Portrait.* Sierra Club Books, San Francisco.

Motion Picture Association of America
2007 Entertainment Industry Market Statistics, 2007. Electronic document, http://www.mpaa.org/USEntertainmentIndustryMarketStats.pdf, accessed September, 2009.

Nielsen Media Research
2009 Three Screen Report: Television, Internet and Mobile Usage in the U.S. Electronic document, http://www.nielsonmedia.com, accessed September, 2011.

Nielsen Wire
2009 The State of the Video Gamer: PC Game and Video Game Console Usage, Fourth Quarter 2008. Electronic document, http://blog.nielsen.com/nielsenwire/, accessed August, 2011.

2012 Consumer Media Usage Across TV, Online, Mobile and Social. Electronic document, http://blog.nielsen.com/nielsenwire/online_mobile/report-consumer-media-usage-across-tv-online-mobile-and-social/, accessed January, 2012.

Ochs, Elinor, Anthony P. Graesch, Angela Mittman, Thomas Bradbury, and Rena Repetti
2006 Video Ethnography and Ethnoarchaeological Tracking. In *The Work-Family Handbook: Multi-Disciplinary Perspectives and Approaches to Research,* edited by Marcie Pitt-Catsouphes, Ellen Ernst Kossek, and Stephen Sweet, pp. 387–409. Lawrence Erlbaum Associates, Mahwah, New Jersey.

Ochs, Elinor, Clotilde Pontecorvo, and Alessandra Fasulo
1996 Socializing Taste. *Ethnos* 61(1–2):7–46.

Ochs, Elinor, Merav Shohet, Belinda Campos, and Margaret E. Beck
2010 Coming Together for Dinner: A Study of Working Families. In *Workplace Flexibility: Realigning 20th-Century Jobs for a 21st-Century Workforce,* edited by Kathleen Christensen and Barbara Schneider, pp. 57–70. Cornell University Press, Ithaca, New York.

Orlando, Angela
2010 Counting Taste as Cultural Capital: Variable Decorative Material Culture in 32 Urban Houses. Working Paper #90. Center on Everyday Lives of Families at UCLA, Los Angeles.

Owens, Bill
1973 *Suburbia.* Fotofolio, New York.

Pigeron, Elisa
2009 The Technology-Mediated Worlds of American Families. Unpublished Ph.D. dissertation, Department of Applied Linguistics, University of California, Los Angeles.

Poirot, Luis
1990 *Pablo Neruda: Absence and Presence.* Translation by Alastair Reid. W.W. Norton, New York.

Rathje, William L.
1979 Modern Material Culture Studies. *Advances in Archaeological Method and Theory* 2:1–37.

1981 A Manifesto for Modern Material-Culture Studies. In *Modern Material Culture: The Archaeology of Us,* edited by Richard A. Gould and Michael B. Schiffer, pp. 51–56. Academic Press, New York.

Rathje, William L., and Cullen Murphy
1992 *Rubbish! The Archaeology of Garbage.* HarperCollins, New York.

Rideout, Victoria, and Elizabeth Hamel
2006 The Media Family: Electronic Media in the Lives of Infants, Toddlers, Preschoolers and Their Parents. Electronic document, www.kff.org/entmedia/upload/7500.pdf, accessed August, 2011. The Henry J. Kaiser Family Foundation.

Ritzer, George
2004 *The McDonaldization of Society.* Pine Forge Press, Thousand Oaks, California.

Robinson, John R., and Geoffrey Godbey
1997 *Time for Life: The Surprising Ways Americans Use Their Time.* Pennsylvania State University Press, University Park.

Rybczynski, Witold
1986 *Home: A Short History of an Idea.* Viking, New York.

Samuelrich, Leslie
2010 Despite Spending Billions on Advertising, the Fast Food Industry Blames Parents for Skyrocketing Obesity Rates. Electronic document, http://www.alternet.org/story/148544/despite_spending_billions_on_advertising%2C_the_fast_food_industry_blames_parents_for_skyrocketing_obesity_rates, accessed October, 2010.

Saxbe, Darby, Anthony P. Graesch, and Marie Alvik
2011 Television as a Social or Solo Activity: Understanding Families' Everyday Television Viewing Patterns. In *Communication Research Reports* 28(2):180–189.

Saxbe, Darby, and Rena L. Repetti
2010 No Place Like Home: Home Tours Predict Daily Patterns of Mood and Cortisol. *Personality and Social Psychology Bulletin* 36(1):71–81.

Saxbe, Darby, Rena Repetti, and Anthony P. Graesch
2011 Time Spent in Housework and Leisure: Links with Parents' Physiological Recovery from Work. *Journal of Family Psychology* 25(2):271–281.

Schiffer, Michael B.
1987 *Formation Processes of the Archaeological Record.* University of Utah Press, Salt Lake City.

Schiffer, Michael B. (with Andrea Miller)
1999 *The Material Life of Human Beings: Artifacts, Behavior, and Communication.* Routledge, New York.

Schlosser, Eric
2001 *Fast Food Nation: The Dark Side of the All-American Meal.* Houghton Mifflin, Boston.

Schmitt, Kelly L., Kimberly Duyck Woolf, and Daniel R. Anderson
2003 Viewing the Viewers: Viewing Behaviors by Children and Adults During Television Programs and Commercials. *Journal of Communication* 53:265–281.

Schor, Juliet B.
1991 *The Overworked American: The Unexpected Decline of Leisure.* Basic, New York.

2004 *Born to Buy: The Commercialized Child and the New Consumer Culture.* Scribner, New York.

Self Storage Association
2011 Self Storage Association Fact Sheet. Electronic document, http://www.selfstorage.org/SSA/Home/AM/ContentManagerNet/ContentDisplay.aspx?Section=Home&ContentID=4228, accessed March, 2011.

Shagawat, Robert
2011 Early Electronic Television: Television Recording—The Origins and Earliest Surviving Live TV Broadcast Recordings. Electronic document, http://www.earlytelevision.org/tv_recordings_the_origins.html, accessed August, 2011. Early Television Museum.

Smith, Aaron
2010 Mobile Access 2010. Pew Internet and American Life Project Report. Electronic document, http://pewinternet.org/Reports/2010/Mobile-Access-2010.aspx, accessed September, 2011. Pew Research Center.

Stearns, Peter N.
2006 *Consumerism in World History: The Global Transformation of Desire.* Routledge, New York.

Taylor, Paul, and Wendy Wang
2010 The Fading Glory of the Television and Telephone. Pew Social and Demographic Trends Report. Electronic document, http://pewresearch.org/pubs/1702/luxury-necessity-television-landline-cell-phone, accessed September, 2011. Pew Research Center.

Thomas, Belia
2003 What the World's Poor Watch on TV. *World Press Review* 50(3). Electronic document, http://www.worldpress.org/Europe/947.cfm, accessed September, 2011.

Thornton, Peter
1984 *Authentic Decor: The Domestic Interior, 1620–1920.* Viking, New York.

Tolin, David F., Randy O. Frost, and Gail Steketee
2007 *Buried in Treasures: Help for Compulsive Acquiring, Saving, and Hoarding.* Oxford University Press, New York.

U.S. Bureau of the Census
1997 American Housing Survey for the Los Angeles-Long Beach Metropolitan Area in 1995. Current Housing Reports H170/95-7. U.S. Department of Housing and Urban Development.

1999 Historical National Population Estimates: July 1, 1900 to July 1, 1999. Electronic document, http://www.census.gov/population/estimates/nation/popclockest.txt, accessed August, 2011. Population Estimates Program, Population Division.

2002 American Fact Finder Quick Report, Sector 44: Retail Trade. Electronic document, http://factfinder.census.gov/home/saff/main.html?_lang=en, accessed September, 2009.

2008a Survey of Residential Alterations and Repairs: Table 4-1, Expenditures for Owner-Occupied One-Unit Properties by Year Built. Electronic document, http://www.census.gov/construction/c50/table_4.pdf, accessed December, 2011.

2008b Survey of Residential Alterations and Repairs: Table S-1, Expenditures of Type of Job, Owner-Occupied Properties: 1994 to 2007. Electronic document, http://www.census.gov/construction/c50/table_s1_0.pdf, accessed December, 2011.

2010 Table 1: Preliminary Annual Estimates of the Resident Population for the United States, Regions, States, and Puerto Rico: April 1, 2000 to July 1, 2010 (NST-PEST2010-01). Electronic document, http://www.census.gov/popest/eval-estimates/eval-est2010.html, accessed August, 2011. Population Estimates Program, Population Division.

U.S. Department of Commerce
2006 U.S. Department of Commerce Industry Outlook: Dolls, Toys, Games, and Children's Vehicles NAICS Code 33993. Electronic document, http://trade.gov/td/ocg/outlook06_toys.pdf, accessed June, 2009.

Vandewater, Elizabeth A., David S. Bickham, and J.H. Lee
2006 Time Well Spent? Relating Television Use to Children's Free-Time Activities. *Pediatrics* 117:181–191.

Veblen, Thorstein
1899 *The Theory of the Leisure Class: An Economic Study in the Evolution of Institutions*. MacMillan, New York.

Warren, Elizabeth
2006 The Middle Class on the Precipice: Rising Financial Risks for American Families. *Harvard Magazine* January–February: 28–31.

Whybrow, Peter C.
2005 *American Mania: When More Is Not Enough*. W.W. Norton, New York.

York, Emily
2011 More Families Warm Up to Frozen Dinners. *Los Angeles Times* 18 March.